AS/A-uide

Marian Cox

Captain Corelli's Mandolin

Louis de Bernières

Philip Allan Updates
Market Place
Deddington
Oxfordshire
OX15 0SE
Tel: 01869 338652
Fax: 01869 337590
e-mail: sales@philipallan.co.uk
www.philipallan.co.uk

Printed by Raithby, Lawrence & Co Ltd, Leicester

P00142

Contents

Introduction

Aims of the guide

The purpose of this Student Text Guide to Louis de Bernières' best-selling novel *Captain Corelli's Mandolin* is to enable you to organise your thoughts and responses to the novel, to deepen your understanding of key feature and aspects, and finally to help you to address the particular requirements of examination questions in order to obtain the best possible grade. It will also prove useful to those of you writing a coursework piece on the novel by providing a number of summaries, lists, analyses and references to help with the content and construction of the assignment. Page references throughout are to the 1999 Vintage edition of the text (earlier editions have different page numbering).

It is assumed that you have read and studied the novel already under the guidance of a teacher or lecturer. This is a revision guide, not an introduction, although some of its content serves the purpose of providing initial background. It can be read in its entirety in one sitting, or it can be dipped into and used as a reference guide to specific and separate aspects of the novel.

The remainder of this Introduction section consists of exam board specifications and Assessment Objectives, which summarise in detail the requirements of the various boards and their schemes of assessment, and a revision scheme which gives a suggested programme for using the material in the guide.

The Text Guidance section consists of a series of chapters which examine key aspects of the book including contexts, interpretations and controversies.

The final section, Questions and Answers, includes mark schemes, model essay plans and some examples of marked work.

Exam board specifications

Captain Corelli's Mandolin is currently on the specifications of the following examination boards:

Edexcel	English Literature A2 Unit 4a/4b (open book examination or coursework)
OCR	English Literature A2 Unit 2712 (open book examination or coursework)
AQA **Spec A**	English Literature A2 Module 5 (comparative text; open book examination or coursework — the book must be compared with Joseph Heller's *Catch 22* under the topic title *Humorous Writing* in the category *Ways of Telling*).

Candidates for Edexcel and OCR examinations will be set two questions on *Captain Corelli's Mandolin* of which they must answer one. The questions will require a response to an aspect of the whole novel, or to a prescribed passage, or to an extract or extracts selected by the candidate. The novel is acceptable as the Prose Text post-1900 option on all boards.

Assessment Objectives

These have been set by QCA and are common to all boards. The ones relevant to this text are:

AO1	communicate clearly the knowledge, understanding and insight appropriate to literary study, using appropriate terminology and accurate and coherent written expression
AO2ii	respond with knowledge and understanding to literary texts of different types and periods, exploring and commenting on relationships and comparisons between literary texts
AO3	show detailed understanding of the ways in which writers' choices of form, structure and language shape meanings
AO4	articulate independent opinions and judgements, informed by different interpretations of literary texts by other readers
AO5ii	evaluate the significance of cultural, historical and other contextual influences on literary texts and study

This can be summarised as:

AO1	clarity of written communication
AO2	informed personal response in relation to time and genre (literary context)
AO3	the creative literary process (context of writing)
AO4	critical and interpretative response (context of reading)
AO5	evaluation of influences (cultural context)

Captain Corelli's Mandolin has a total weighting of 30%, divided as follows:

Edexcel	Unit 4b: AO1 – 10%; AO3 – 5%; AO4 – 10%; AO5ii – 5%
OCR	Unit 2712: AO1 – 10%; AO2ii – 5%; AO3 – 5%; AO4 – 5%; AO5ii – 5%
AQA (A)	Module 5: AO1 – 5%; AO2ii – 13%; AO3 – 6%; AO4 – 6%

Note the significantly different weighting of the Assessment Objectives between the different examining boards for the same text. It is essential that you pay close attention to the AOs, and their weighting, for the board for which you are entered. These are what the examiner will be looking for, and you must address them *directly* and *specifically*, in addition to proving general familiarity with and understanding of the text, and being able to present an argument clearly, relevantly and convincingly.

Note that the examiners are seeking above all else evidence of an *informed personal response* to the text. A revision guide such as this can help you to understand the text and to form your own opinions, but it cannot replace your own ideas and responses as an individual reader.

Revision advice

For the examined units it is possible that either brief or more extensive revision will be necessary because the original study of the text took place some time previously. It is therefore useful to know how to go about revising and which tried and tested methods are considered the most successful for literature exams at all levels, from GCSE to degree finals.

Below is a guide on how not to do it — think of reasons why not in each case. **Don't**:

- leave it until the last minute
- assume you remember the text well enough and don't need to revise at all
- spend hours designing a beautiful revision schedule
- revise more than one text at the same time
- think you don't need to revise because it is an open book exam
- decide in advance what you think the questions will be and revise only for those
- try to memorise particular essay plans
- reread texts randomly and aimlessly
- revise for longer than 2 hours in one sitting
- miss school lessons in order to work alone at home
- try to learn a whole ring-binder's worth of work
- tell yourself that character and plot revision is enough
- imagine that watching the video again is the best way to revise
- rely on a study guide instead of the text

There are no short-cuts to effective exam revision; the only one way to know a text extremely well, and to know your way around it in an exam, is to have done the necessary studying. If you use the following method, in six easy stages, for both open and closed book revision, you will not only revisit and reassess all your previous work on the text in a manageable way but will be able to distil, organise and retain your knowledge. Don't try to do it all in one go: take regular breaks for refreshment and a change of scene.

(1) Between a month and a fortnight before the exam, depending on your schedule (a simple list of stages with dates displayed in your room, not a work of art!), you will need to reread the text, this time taking stock of all the under-linings and marginal annotations as well. As you read, collect onto sheets of A4 the essential ideas and quotations as you come across them. The acts of selecting key material and recording it as notes are natural ways of stimulating thought and aiding memory.

(2) Reread the highlighted areas and marginal annotations in your critical extracts and background handouts, and add anything useful from them to your list of notes and quotations. Then reread your previous essays and the teacher's comments. As you look back through essays written earlier in the course, you should have the pleasant sensation of realising that you can now write much better on the text than you could then. You will also discover that much of your huge file of notes is redundant or repeated, and that you have changed your mind about some beliefs, so that the distillation process is not too daunting. Selecting what is important is the way to crystallise your knowledge and under-standing.

(3) During the run-up to the exam you need to do lots of practice essay plans to help you identify any gaps in your knowledge and give you practice in planning in 5–8 minutes. Past paper titles for you to plan are provided in this guide, some of which can be done as full timed essays — and marked strictly according to exam criteria — which will show whether length and timing are problematic for you. If you have not seen a copy of a real exam paper before you take your first module, ask to see a past paper so that you are familiar with the layout and rubric.

(4) About a week before the exam, reduce your two or three sides of A4 notes to a double-sided postcard of very small, dense writing. Collect a group of keywords by once again selecting and condensing, and use abbreviations for quotations (first and last word), and character and place names (initials). (For the comparison unit your postcard will need to refer to key points, themes and quotations in both texts relevant to the specific theme or genre topic.) The act of choosing and writing out the short quotations will help you to focus on the essential issues, and to recall them quickly in the exam. Make sure that your selection covers the main themes and includes examples of symbolism, style, comments on character, examples of irony, point of view or other significant

aspects of the text. Previous class discussion and essay writing will have indicated which quotations are useful for almost any title; pick those which can serve more than one purpose, for instance those which reveal character and theme, and are also an example of language. In this way a minimum number of quotations can have maximum application.

(5) You now have in a compact, accessible form all the material for any possible essay title. There are only half a dozen themes relevant to a literary text so if you have covered these you should not meet with any nasty surprises when you read the exam questions. You do not need to refer to your file of paperwork again, or even to the text. For the few days before the exam, you can read through your handy postcard whenever and wherever you get the opportunity. Each time you read it, which will only take a few minutes, you are reminding yourself of all the information you will be able to recall in the exam to adapt to the general title or to support an analysis of particular passages.

(6) A fresh, active mind works wonders, and information needs time to settle, so don't try to cram just before the exam. Relax the night before and get a good night's sleep. Then you will be able to enter the exam room with all the confidence of a well-prepared candidate.

Coursework

The coursework writing process differs from final examinations in being more leisurely and more supported by the discussion and drafting stages, but the issues of the novel remain the same, as does the need for a relevant, focused response. The requirement is a total of 2,000–2,500 words as a single study, or two pieces of approximately 1,250 words each. One of them may be a creative assignment, which 'must be accompanied by the candidate's critical commentary, explaining the rationale and the textual basis of the assignment'. As with the exam essay, 'students' work must be informed by different interpretations of their text by other readers.'

Coursework should be word-processed in the interests of presentation, consideration for the examiner, and ease of alteration for the student. There are number of key stages in the coursework writing process:

- Once your title is decided and you are familiar with the Assessment Objectives, reread the novel and all the notes and annotations you have made, extracting what is relevant for your title.
- With teacher guidance, read some background material and critical essays, and collect any relevant information from them. Keep a list of the books and articles you have consulted. Rephrase any ideas you borrow from elsewhere.
- Write a one-page essay plan, consisting of sub-headings and main points, and

show it to your teacher to ensure you have covered the title fully and have adopted an appropriate essay structure.

- Write a draft of the essay, roughly the right length, based on your plan. Use details, examples and quotations form the text to support your points.
- Read through the draft, making sure that you have answered fully and remained focused on the question. Submit your draft to your teacher in good time.
- When your draft is returned, put into practice the comments offered to help you improve your essay and its grade, and adjust the length if necessary.
- Produce the final version, improving content, expression and accuracy where possible. Check the final word count. Include a bibliography listing the texts you have quoted from or consulted in the writing of your essay.
- After a final read through, putting yourself in the position of the reader, make last-minute adjustments and submit your essay — before the deadline.

Writing examination essays

Essay content

One of the key skills you are being asked to demonstrate at A-level is the ability to select and tailor your knowledge of the text and its background to the question set in the exam paper. In order to reach the highest levels, you need to avoid 'pre-packaged' essays which lack focus, relevance and coherence, and which simply contain everything you know about the text. Be ruthless in rejecting irrelevant material, after considering whether it can be made relevant by a change of emphasis. Aim to cover the whole question, not just part of it; your response needs to demonstrate breadth and depth, covering the full range of text elements: character, event, theme and language. Only half a dozen approaches are possible for any set text, though they may be phrased in a variety of ways, and they are likely to refer to the key themes of the text. Preparation of the text therefore involves extensive discussion and practice at manipulating these core themes so that there should be no surprises in the exam. An apparently new angle is more likely to be something familiar presented in an unfamiliar way and you should not panic or reject the choice of question because you think you know nothing about it.

Exam titles are open-ended in the sense that there is not an obvious right answer, and you would therefore be unwise to give a dismissive, extreme or entirely one-sided response. The question would not have been set if the answer were not debatable. An ability and willingness to see both sides is an Assessment Objective and shows independence of judgement as a reader. Do not be afraid to explore the issues and do not try to tie the text into one neat interpretation. If there is ambiguity it is likely to be deliberate on the part of the author and must be discussed; literary texts are complex and often paradoxical, and it would be a misreading of them to suggest that there is only one possible interpretation. You are not expected, however, to argue equally strongly or extensively for both sides of an argument, since personal opinion is an important factor. It is advisable to deal with the alternative view at the beginning of your response, and then construct your own view as the main part of the essay. This makes it less likely that you will appear to cancel out your own line of argument.

Choosing the right question

The first skill you must show when presented with the exam paper is the ability to choose the better, for you, of the two questions on your text where there is a choice. This is not to say you should always go for the same type of essay (whole-text or passage-based) and if the question is not one which you feel happy with for any reason, you should seriously consider the other, even if it is not the type you normally prefer. It is unlikely but possible that a question contains a word you are not sure you know the meaning of, in which case it would be safer to choose the other one.

Do not be tempted to choose a question because of its similarity to one you have already done. Freshness and thinking on the spot usually produce a better product than attempted recall of a previous essay which may have received only a mediocre mark in the first place. The exam question is unlikely to have exactly the same focus and your response may seem 'off centre' as a result, as well as stale and perfunctory in expression. Essay questions fall into the following categories: close section analysis and relation to whole text; characterisation; setting and atmosphere; structure and effectiveness; genre; language and style; themes and issues. Remember, however, that themes are relevant to all essays and that analysis, not just description, is always required.

Once you have decided which exam question to attempt, follow the procedure below for whole-text and passage-based, open- and closed-book essays.

(1) Underline all the key words in the question and note how many parts the question has.

(2) Plan your answer, using aspects of the key words and parts of the question as sub-headings, in addition to themes. Aim for 10–12 ideas. Check that the Assessment Objectives are covered.

(3) Support your argument by selecting the best examples of characters, events, imagery and quotations to prove your points. Remove ideas for which you can find no evidence.

(4) Structure your answer by grouping and numbering your points in a logical progression. Identify the best general point to keep for the conclusion.

(5) Introduce your essay with a short paragraph setting the context and defining the key words in the question as broadly, but relevantly, as possible.

(6) Write the rest of the essay, following your structured plan but adding extra material if it occurs to you. Paragraph your writing and consider expression, especially sentence structure and vocabulary choices, as you write. Signal changes in the direction of your argument with paragraph openers such as 'Furthermore' and 'However'. Use plenty of short, integrated quotations and use the words of the text rather than your own where possible. Use technical terms appropriately, and write concisely and precisely, avoiding vagueness and ambiguity.

(7) Your conclusion should sound conclusive and make it clear that you have answered the question. It should be an overview of the question and the text, not a repetition or a summary of points already made.

(8) Cross out your plan with a neat diagonal line.

(9) Check your essay for content, style, clarity and accuracy. With neat crossings-out, correct errors of fact, spelling, grammar and punctuation. Improve expression if possible, and remove any repetition and irrelevance. Add clarification and missing evidence, if necessary, using omission marks or asterisks. Even at this stage, good new material can be added.

There is no such thing as a perfect or model essay; flawed essays can gain full marks. There is always something more which could have been said, and examiners realise that students have limitations when writing under pressure in timed conditions. You are not penalised for what you didn't say in comparison to some idealised concept of the answer, but rewarded for the knowledge and understanding you have shown. It is not as difficult as you may think to do well, provided that you are familiar with the text and have sufficient essay-writing experience. If you follow the above process and **underline**, **plan**, **support**, **structure**, **write** and **check**, you can't go far wrong.

Text Guidance

Contexts

Assessment Objective 5 requires the candidate to 'evaluate the significance of cultural, historical and other contextual influences on literary texts'. There are a number of contexts within which *Captain Corelli's Mandolin* may be viewed.

It is important to remember, however, that a novel is a work of fiction, not of history, and although many readers have criticised the book over the inaccuracy of historical details, this is not relevant to an assessment of the book as literature. On the other hand, as a work set in an identifiable historical context, it is legitimate to examine the use the author has made of historical material to create his fictional world. The distinction is, of course, muddied by the author's introduction of so many real historical figures — actually treating them as characters — and it could be argued that this creates a greater expectation that the historical aspects will be reliable. Again, there are other examples of authors who have used (or, arguably, traduced) real historical characters in this way.

Historical and political context

There are a number of historical contexts in the novel, and they all play important roles in establishing the setting and the mood of the action. The novel is set on the Greek island of Cephallonia, and covers a substantial slice of the history of the island in the twentieth century, including war, occupation, civil war, earthquake and profound social change; it touches upon the wider history of Greece during the 53 years which it covers. It also deals extensively with the Greek role and experience during the Second World War, and particularly with the experience of occupation by the Italians and the Germans.

Greece

The novel gives a convincing depiction of traditional village life on an Ionian island between 1940 and 1993. It chronicles the resilience of this way of life in the face of war and natural disaster, and its undermining by the advent of mass tourism from the 1980s onwards, which has ironically been exacerbated by the publication of the novel and the filming of it in Cephallonia. De Bernières' depiction of the Greek Civil War is by far the most contentious aspect of the novel: he has been virulently criticised in Greece and Cephallonia over this aspect of the book, and he agreed to remove an offending paragraph of the book relating to the Communist *andartes* for the Greek-language edition. Although all the behaviours which he describes undoubtedly occurred, his account is one-sided: there *were* members of ELAS who fought the occupying forces, and the other resistance armies were not blameless. Nevertheless, de Bernières is right to emphasise that far more Greeks were killed by other Greeks during the Civil War than by German soldiers during the occupation, and certainly atrocities were regularly committed — by both sides.

Since de Bernières spent only a fortnight on holiday in Cephallonia and wrote the novel subsequently in Britain, he had to rely on the accounts, inevitably partial, of Greeks living in London. Ironically, the political furore caused by the novel proves its main thesis, which is that it is impossible for everyone to reach agreement on historical events.

Mussolini and Italian fascism

Benito Mussolini was the creator of the political philosophy fascism, named after the Roman *fasces,* a bundle of sticks which was a symbol of power and authority. Originally a socialist, his experiences during the First World War convinced him of the importance of nationalism, and in the years following the war he created a movement based upon violence and patriotism. Swept to power in 1922, fascism was a movement of slogans rather than substance and was characterised principally by corruption and incompetence; despite popular belief, the trains did *not* run on time in fascist Italy! Two of the more famous slogans illustrate Mussolini's ideas:

> *Mussolini is always right!*
> *Believe! Obey! Fight!*

Although Mussolini represented war as the highest human activity ('I love war!' he once said), he did not manage to prepare properly for it. When the regime became unpopular in the mid-1930s he turned to aggression to distract attention from domestic problems. The invasion of Abyssinia was achieved by aerial bombing and the use of poison gas; the subsequent invasion of Albania, an ally of Italy, was a fiasco which was successful only because the Albanians had no armed forces.

Adolf Hitler, the Nazi leader in Germany, initially modelled his movement in part on Italian fascism, and after some initial suspicion the two formed an alliance (the Axis Pact) in 1936. It was always expected that Italy would parti-cipate in the coming war, although her armed forces were manifestly unprepared when it broke out in September 1939.

The Second World War

As resistance to the Nazi German *blitzkrieg* (lightning war) in Europe crumbled in the summer of 1940, Mussolini feared that Italy might miss the war. He therefore launched an ill-fated invasion of France in June, attacked the British in Libya in September and on 28 October invaded Greece from Albania. In a bitter war fought in atrociously cold conditions in the Albanian mountains, the Greeks more or less defeated the Italians; the Germans intervened in April 1940 to save Mussolini from humiliation and conquered Greece within 3 weeks. The novel is accurate in its depiction of the war and the attitude of the Greeks to the arrival of the Italian occupation forces.

As far as the occupation is concerned, Greece was unusual but not unique in being occupied both by the Italians and by the Germans, and much of the interest in the book derives from the contrast between the attitudes and behaviours of the two occupying powers as depicted by de Bernières. Some readers have criticised the portrayal of the Italians as unhistorical, pointing out that they could be cruel occupiers and that they engaged in reprisals much as the Germans did. Recent research, however, on the analagous occupation of Nice in France, another place subjected to occupation by the two Axis powers, strongly reinforces the picture given in the novel of Italian occupiers friendly to the local people and treated with indulgent contempt by them. The two peoples have similar temperaments and cultures, and after the Italians changed sides they shared a common enemy with the Greeks. Italians returning to Cephallonia are still greeted fondly by elderly locals.

In the years immediately preceding the war, the young males of all combatant countries were conscripted for military service, although individuals could volunteer first, as Mandras definitely does. Corelli and Weber, as officers, may also have chosen to join rather than be conscripted later as enlisted men, and Carlo probably volunteered for the army as being a preferable all-male environment. The slaughter of the Italians by the German army in September 1943, the dramatic heart of the novel, is entirely historically accurate and was one of the most horrific events of the war. Here, as elsewhere (see, for example, Metaxas in ch. 5), however, considerable caution should be exercised in evaluating those passages in which de Bernières fictionalises the thoughts and actions of historical personages in real historical events.

The Greek Civil War

The monarchy in Greece was already unpopular for having supported the semi-fascist dictatorship of Metaxas for some years prior to the outbreak of war; the Communists (ELAS) played a dominant role in the organisation of resistance to the occupation, but certainly spent more of their time and energy fighting against the rival monarchist force (EDES) than against the occupiers, despite the best efforts of British Special Operations Executive (SOE) agents to make them work together. The only real achievement of SOE was the destruction of the Gorgopotamos railway viaduct by ELAS and EDES fighters, referred to in ch. 32.

At the end of the war, the king returned, with the direct support of Winston Churchill, the British Prime Minister, but probably against the wishes of the majority of the population. The second civil war broke out in 1947 and lasted until 1949, when the Communists were finally defeated; it was marked by extraordinary brutality on both sides. It remains a very bitter and divisive subject in Greece to this day, not least because, after a democratic interlude, a right-wing military dictatorship again ruled in Greece between 1967 and 1974, and a stable democracy was only achieved after its overthrow.

Cultural context

The novel paints an attractive picture of the traditional life of a Greek island village, especially just before the outbreak of war. On the whole, de Bernières gives a reliable and fair impression of this society, although the authenticity of a number of details has been challenged. It is important to be aware of, and to evaluate, the ways in which the author has used this social structure to give a framework of values and expectations for the characters and the action. To enable the reader to get the full picture and flavour of the Mediterranean setting, and to appreciate some of the ironies and anomalies of the behaviour and beliefs of certain characters, below are some general points to bear in mind, some of which apply to Italian as well as to Greek society, and many of which still apply today in the Greek islands.

Mothers and sons

This is regarded as the strongest bond in the Greek family, and has religious echoes of the Madonna and child. Mothers traditionally forgive their sons anything, and take their side against anyone. Drosoula, unusually, always wanted a daughter. Mandras commits suicide after his mother, not Pelagia, rejects him; her curse is unexpected, unbearable, and the equivalent of withdrawing his right to life. If a woman never has a son, like Pelagia, she has been deprived of her main function in life, which is to provide a male heir and give him the name of his father's father.

Daughters and dowries

Girls were not considered to be equal with boys and the father was offered commiserations instead of congratulations for the birth of a female child. For this reason the dowry system existed, whereby a daughter had to have something to offer her prospective husband as well as herself. If a sum of money was not forthcoming, then at least a plot of land or a herd of goats would be expected, as well as a set of hand-embroidered household linen. Dr Iannis refuses to provide Pelagia with a dowry, which causes consternation to Mandras and provokes his need to prove himself a hero. Women at that time could not expect to become self-supporting financially by training for a career or taking work outside the home. They did not travel beyond the domestic sphere of cooking, sewing and general house-keeping, even to the local coffee shop, which was an exclusively male preserve — hence Pelagia's frustration at 'having been born into the wrong world' with no possibility of being able to study medicine. Men, on the other hand, tended to be defined by their job, e.g. the priest, the shepherd, the soldier.

The motherland and the Virgin Mary

In Greek, Greece is a feminine noun, and the Virgin Mary is a very important figure in the Greek Orthodox church, with a name day on 15 August, as in Catholic Italy. Pelagia, who retains her virginity throughout the book, represents the island of Cephallonia and Greece generally; her sufferings, losses and violations are theirs. Though unmarried, she becomes a mother and a grand-mother. Her name refers to a saint who was a virgin of Antioch and whose name day is 8 October. When Mandras goes off to fight against the Italians in Albania, he worships the conflated female images of Pelagia, the motherland and the Virgin. The three types of love — erotic, patriotic, religious — have been a feature of Greek literature since Homer.

The pastoral and the Olympian

The word 'pastoral' means 'of shepherds' and refers to the myth of idyllic rural life, typified by laughter, courtship and community spirit, which goes back to the golden age of classical Greece, when it was referred to as 'Arcadia' or 'Arcady'. Village life on the beautiful hillside of Cephallonia revolves around a harmonious natural existence of living off the land and sea by fishing, growing herbs and olives, and keeping goats and poultry. The rhythms of the seasons are celebrated and punctuated by ritual feasting and dancing, wine and song. This way of life, unchanged since Homeric times, is destroyed first by the German occupation and then by the earthquake. Finally, the islanders become dependent on the gods of commerce and tourism.

Alekos, the shepherd on the top of Mt Aenos, high above the world on an island 'filled with gods', has the detachment of the immortals, unconcerned and untouched by either domestic concerns or the earth-shattering events of politics, history and war. He is a quasi-mythological figure in the novel, agelessly enduring all seasons and all changes. With his remote and lofty viewpoint, he has the 'grandeur and impartiality' Dr Iannis is looking for as a historical voice for his Personal History.

Saints and superstitions

Greeks take their many saints very seriously as a latter-day replacement for the ancient pantheon. Every church is dedicated to a particular saint and each village or island has a local saint whose relics or icon are believed to be capable of working miracles, as in the case of St Gerasimos. All orthodox Greeks must be baptised and given the name of a saint. Dr Iannis, with his healing gift, is a saintly figure throughout the novel because of his wisdom, tolerance and martyrdom. Other miracle-performing or heroic characters also play saintly roles. Generally, the Greeks could be described as a superstitious people — for instance, they believe in the Evil Eye — who attempt to ward off misfortune or attract fortune by the performance of gestures, the utterance of set phrases, and the use of particular greetings for specific occasions.

Barbarians and civil war

In 189 BC the Romans invaded Greece and conquered it for the first time. Thereafter, a seemingly endless succession of less civilised foreign armies claimed and robbed the cradle of democracy and learning. Cavafy, a famous Greek poet living in Alexandria, wrote a well-known poem called 'Waiting for the Barbarians', naming a chronic national fear. However, because there is a theory that there are two aspects to the psyche of every Greek — the Hellene who respects reason and the Romaios who lets the heart rule the head — civil war could be viewed as an inevitable eventual consequence, and a horror even more destructive than an external threat. As Dr Iannis says: 'In the past we had the barbarians. Now we have only ourselves to blame.' Greeks today have not forgiven or forgotten the atrocities of the civil war or the allegiance of each area or even family, both sides accusing the other of barbarism.

Burial and resurrection

Since ancient times funeral ritual and a belief in the afterlife has been sacred to the Greeks. The most important event in the Greek religious and family calendar is Easter, the celebration of the Resurrection, and the phoenix, a mythical, immortal bird which arises anew from its own ashes, is a potent literary and political symbol (adopted by the Greek dictatorship of 1967–1974). Various characters, alive and dead or presumed dead, come back from the grave or make a ghostly reappearance in the novel, thereby acquiring mythical status.

August and October

These two months, referred to many times in the novel, are significant for Greece generally and for Cephallonia in particular. The two feast days of St Gerasimos occur in August and October, and 28 October is the date on which Metaxas in effect declared war on Italy. The feast day of the Virgin Mary is on 15 August, and the earthquake occurred in August 1953. These two months act as a framework for all the personal and historical anniversaries which lend structure to the novel and to the memories of the characters.

Honour and shame

Philotimo, love of honour, is a revered and ancient heroic concept in the mind of Greeks, the other side of the same coin being shame. Fighting for your country, for instance, is honourable, but betraying your friends is shameful. Dr Iannis and Corelli follow a personal code of honour which prevents them from committing an unworthy act, whereas Mandras must die for bringing disgrace on his mother, and Weber is treated with contempt for his treachery. An honourable death is distinctly preferable to a shameful life in Mediterranean cultures. Corelli shows how he would have faced death honourably in his message to Appollonio and his demeanour in the face of the firing squad. Honour entails risk, however, and Corelli endangers his own and members of his battery's lives by taking an honourable stand against the duplicitous Germans, having been let down by the incompetence of the Italian commander, General Gandin.

Sea and mountain

These are the twin features of island and mainland coastal landscape in a country which has few rivers or forests but is famously beautiful. Homer had a lot to say about the 'wine-dark sea' and the 'violet-crowned mountains'. The images of sea and mountain occur repeatedly in the Bible, in Greek Orthodox rites and in classical and modern Greek poetry, song and drama. Pelagia's name means 'ocean woman'. The mountains are the home of the Olympian gods, and the frontier for the defence of the homeland. Greeks have regarded themselves as a sea-going nation of adventurers and fishermen since before *The Odyssey*, and have respect for the mystical significance of the ocean. Both sea and mountain have their part to play in the novel, personally and politically, repelling or bringing invaders, and associated with life and death.

Mythology

The mythological context of *Captain Corelli's Mandolin* is discussed on pages 52–55, but in a broader sense Greek mythology pervades the book; Greek gods and heroes are alluded to, and de Bernières often assumes that the reader will understand the reference. In this he does no more than reflect the reality of life in Greece then and now: the stories and characters of Greek mythology are intimately familiar to the people and form a constant background and frame of reference for their daily life. Classical myths, until comparatively recently, formed a common body of knowledge for all educated Europeans, along with familiarity with Latin and Ancient Greek language. There is a story, which de Bernières does not include presumably because he does not know it (though he would approve of it if he did), about the German occupation of Crete at the time in which the novel is set: when a British SOE officer succeeded in capturing and abducting the German commanding general on Crete, they woke one morning on Mount

Ida and were both able to recite in Latin an ode about that mountain by the Roman poet Horace. This showed them how much they had in common despite the temporary divisions imposed by war, and they went on to become lifelong friends.

Dr Iannis makes extensive reference to Greek mythological characters throughout the novel. It is not necessary to know the myths referred to in any detail, though it is useful to know what each god represents (see p. 49 below).

The end of the novel has a metaphorical depiction of the **Three Fates** of classical Greek mythology. This suggests that Fate has been presiding over the novel throughout, finally bringing the lovers together again. The three women wearing white, like Greek goddesses, can be said to represent the future, the present and the past. One is looking forward, one is looking in a mirror and the third is facing backwards immersed in a newspaper, i.e. an ephemeral record of history (and one threatened by the breeze). Modern and ancient, reality and imagination, are synthesised in the vision of the 'liberty and beauty' of the girls and of Greece on the 'venerable grey moped', travelling through time — an inspiration to Corelli for his next concerto, to celebrate the 'eternal spirit of Greece'.

The island of Cephallonia

Cephallonia (which is more often spelt with one 'l') is, by legend, named after Cephalus, an Athenian who was exiled after, perhaps inadvertently, killing his wife Procris. One of his great-grandsons was Odysseus, hero of *The Odyssey*, who is generally thought to have lived on neighbouring Ithaca, although one school of thought believes he lived on Cephallonia. In Homer's epic he was guarded by Cephallonian giants and Cephallonian pine-trees were used to build his ships, so the connection is strong.

The island has been occupied since at least 4000 BC and artefacts from this period have been found in several places. Myceneans from the mainland settled from about 1400 BC and developed a substantial civilisation. This was the historical period of the Trojan War and *The Odyssey*. From 1100 BC the island was invaded by Dorians and little is known until the period of the Athenian Golden Age in about 500 BC. Cephallonia was involved in various wars during the ensuing 300 years until the Romans occupied the island in 198 BC — the start of nearly 2,150 years of intermittent Italian occupation which ended only in 1943.

In the early centuries of the Christian era the Roman Empire came under increasing pressure from barbarian invasions from the east, and in 285 AD the Empire divided into two. The Western empire fell to the barbarians in 476, but the Eastern Empire, of which Cephallonia was part, survived as the Christian Byzantine Empire, with its capital at Constantinople and under Greek cultural domination. Orthodox Christianity was established as the religion of the people, and in 887 the island became the administrative capital of the Ionian islands.

In 1081 the Normans under Robert Guiscard arrived and brought Roman Catholic Christianity with them; Fiskardo is named after a version of Guiscard's name. During the next century Cephallonia changed hands several times between the Byzantine Empire, the Normans, the Genoese and the Venetians. In 1194 the Venetian Orsini family gained control and abolished the Orthodox church. Following the Sack of Constantinople in 1204 in the spectacularly misdirected Fourth Crusade, when westerners took over all of the Greek possessions of the Byzantine Empire, Cephallonia became part of the Kingdom of the Morea. The island remained in the hands of wealthy Venetian families for three centuries: the Orsini family from 1195 to 1356, and the Tocchi from 1357 to 1484. Leonardo, the last of the Tocchi, restored the Orthodox Church but was forced to hand Cephallonia over to the Ottoman Turks, who had captured Constantinople in 1453 and were consolidating their hold over all of Greece and the Balkans. On Cephallonia, though, Turkish rule was to prove short-lived: Venice invaded in 1500 and regained control of the island. Despite occasional raids by Turkish pirates, this was to be the longest period of stable government, lasting nearly three centuries to 1797.

In 1797, by the terms of the Treaty of Campo Formio, France took over the territories of the Venetian Republic including Cephallonia. The old Italian aristocratic families lost their rights and possessions. In 1799 the French were expelled by a Russo-Turkish coalition and the island was briefly restored to the Ottoman Empire. The French reoccupied the island between 1807 and 1809 but did not formally annex it, and were displaced by the British in October 1809. The Congress of Vienna confirmed British possession in 1815 and all the Ionian islands became a British Protectorate between 1815 and 1864.

In 1821 the Greek War of Independence began, and the Kingdom of Greece was finally established in May 1832. With the passing of time it became increasingly anomalous for the Ionian islands to be under British control, and there was a movement for union ('Enosis') with Greece which came to fruition in 1864.

Greece had only a tangential involvement in the First World War, but the decision of the Paris Peace Conference to award Rhodes and the Dodecanese islands to Italy was a reminder of continuing Italian interest in the region, and one of the first acts of Mussolini as Italian Prime Minister was to bombard Corfu over a border dispute in 1923.

After the Italian and German occupations of 1941–44 came the Civil War of 1947–49, the earthquake of 1953, which destroyed most of the Venetian architecture of the island, and thereafter, finally, relative peace and increasing prosperity with the relentless growth of tourism from the 1980s onwards. This process has, of course, been dramatically affected by the publicity generated by the novel and, more recently, the making of the film.

The patron saint of Cephallonia is **St Gerasimos** who was born in 1507 at Trikala on the mainland. He lived for 12 years in the Holy Land prior to settling on Cephallonia and setting up a nunnery at Omala. He dedicated his life to good works on behalf of the villagers, dying in 1579. Miracles soon followed, and when his body was exhumed 2 years later it had not decomposed, so he was declared a saint. His feast days are 16 August (the anniversary of his death) and 20 October (the date of his exhumation).

The principal places mentioned in the text

The mandolin, Corelli and Weber

Louis de Bernières is himself a passionate player, maker and exponent of the mandolin and has stated that he hoped the novel would lead to a revival of the instrument — which it has done.

The mandolin is a stringed instrument resembling a lute in shape. It was developed in the fifteenth century out of the medieval mandola and became popular in the eighteenth century when it was employed extensively by composers such as Handel and Mozart. It was first employed as a serious classical instrument by the Italian composer Arcangelo Corelli during the seventeenth century.

Corelli was born in 1653 at Fusignano in Italy, and studied in Bologna before settling in Rome. He was an outstanding violin player and has been described as the father of modern violin technique, but he is best known as a composer. His Concerti Grossi are masterpieces of Baroque orchestral music. He died in 1713 in Rome.

The principal characteristics of the mandolin are its four double strings, giving it a richness of tone. It is played with a plectrum and the swift repetition of notes (tremolo) to overcome the instrument's inability to create sustained sounds gives a very distinctive tone. Compared to a guitar, it has a deep, ribbed body, and its name derives from the Italian for almond, 'mandorla'.

There are several varieties of mandolin. The Neapolitan, with a deep, almond-shaped body, is considered to be the standard design. By contrast, the Portuguese mandolin has a slightly tapered flat back ('It slipped. That's the trouble with these roundbacks from Naples. I often think I should get a Portuguese one with a flat back.') A common feature of mandolins is that the soundboard is *purfled*: thin bands of woods of contrasting colours decorate the edges of the soundhole and the soundboard.

Another musical link between fact and fiction in the novel is Weber's name. **Carl Maria von Weber** was a distinguished Austrian composer (1786–1826) and a cousin of Mozart's wife. He is principally remembered for his operas, of which the best known is *Der Freischütz* (literally, 'The Free-shooter'; 'The Sharp-shooter' or 'The Marksman' are the closest translations). Günter Weber is, of course, also Austrian.

Glossary

Greek

agapeton	beloved
agora	market
ai gamisou	get stuffed (or stronger)
alafranga	in the West European mode
andartes	resistance fighters
apodosis	restitution
apokrea(s)	carnival period, the 2 weeks before Lent
avgolemono	egg and lemon sauce
barba	uncle – familiar term of address for an older man
bravo	used in Greek just as in English
Christopsomo	a kind of Easter bread
divaratiko	a dance
dolmades	stuffed vine leaves
efkharisto	thank you
elephtheria	freedom
enosis	union (with Greece)
exiteia	exile from the Greek homeland
fourno	oven, often communal
fustanella	traditional costume, worn by fustanellophoroi
heston	shit on him
iatre	doctor, when addressed; iatros when referred to
iconostasis	the screen separating the sanctuary from the main body of a church, covered with sacred icons
Kalamatianos	dance from Kalamata in the Peloponnese

kalimera	good morning, good day		mitera	mother
kalispera	good evening		paidia	literally children; used colloquially of boys or girls of the younger generation
kamakia	'harpoons'; young men who offer their sexual services to female tourists			
			panegyri	festival
kapheneion	a coffee shop where only the men of the village pass their time, playing *tavli* (backgammon) and discussing politics		papakis	little father; term of affection used by Pelagia
			papas	father or priest (in Greek, the same thing). Note that this is used incorrectly by de Bernières in ch. 1; the vocative should be *Papa*
katharevousa	a formal and archaic form of modern Greek			
kefi	high spirits			
kleftico	oven-baked lamb dish			
klefts	bandits		patir	formal form of address to a priest
kokkinelli	locally-made red wine		patrida	our country, fatherland/motherland
kokoretsi	dish made of charcoal-grilled lamb intestines			
			peripato(s)	walk
kori	daughter		putanas yie	son of a whore
koritsimou	my little girl		raki	a strong alcoholic drink
kourabiedes	Christmas cookies		rebetika	songs (especially sung and danced in Athenian dives frequented especially by refugees from Asia Minor)
kyria	lady, madam; used respectfully for any woman of marriageable age whether married or not			
kyrie	sir; form of address used to any man		retsina	white wine tasting of pine resin
			robola	the best-known white wine of Cephallonia
loukoumades	a kind of small doughnut, served hot with honey			
			syrtos	a dance
mangas	an affectionate name for a cunning, streetwise person (singular; correctly *manges* in the plural, as used in ch. 9)		theh gamiesei	this should probably read *dhen gamiesai* which is a milder form of *ai gamisou*
			theio(s)	uncle
mayeritsa	soup made from lamb offal, thickened with egg and lemon; eaten at midnight on Easter Eve to break the Lenten fast		tsalimia	a dance
			tsoureki	sweet Easter bread
			vasilopeta	Christmas and New Year cake containing a good-luck coin (correctly *vassilopitta*)
mezedakia	little bites of food as appetisers			

Italian

Italian	English
aiuta(r)mi	help me
aspettami	wait for me
bella bambina	beautiful young girl
bella fanciulla	beautiful young girl
buon giorno	good morning, good day
carogna	carrion, scum
casa nostra	our house
cazzo d'un cane	dog's prick
che succede?	what's happening? what's up?
con brio	with vigour
Ecco una carta della Cephallonia, dov'e Argostoli?	I have a map of Cephallonia, where is Argostoli?
figlio	son
figlio d'un culo	son of an arse-hole
fischio	whistle
Il Duce	The Leader; title adopted by Mussolini as leader of fascist Italy
io son ricco e tu sei bella	I am rich and you are beautiful
Libro e Moschetto – Fascisto Perfetto	'Book and musket – the perfect Fascist' (correctly, Fascista)
merda!	shit!
micino	(cute) little (cat)
panettone	Italian cake, especially for Christmas
Partito e Impero	Party and Empire
pezzo di merda	piece of shit
porco Dio!	God is a pig!
puttana	whore
rompiscatole	pain in the arse
siamo perduti	we are lost
sola, perduta, abandonnata	alone, lost and abandoned (from La Traviata) (correctly abbandonata)
sotto voce	in a low voice, a whisper
sporcaccione	dirty pig (figurative)
supergreccia	the Italian High Command in Greece
tesoro mio	my treasure
testa d'asino	the brains of an ass
va fanculo	fuck off (correctly vaffanculo)
vengo	I'm coming
Vuole fare un giro?	Do you want to come for a ride?

Plot synopsis

The plot of *Captain Corelli's Mandolin* takes place between the summer of 1940 and the autumn of 1993 and is told in 73 chapters. The first 63 take place during the relatively short period from summer 1940 to autumn 1944, leaving ten chapters for the following 49 years.

Although the narrative does not proceed along conventional linear lines, since it changes viewpoint and genre regularly and often back-tracks or over-laps, it is nevertheless possible to group the chapters and events in order to impose some shape on the novel.

Chapters 1–8: village life in Cephallonia; introduction of main Greek characters and political positions; rumours of war; the comic perspective

1 Dr Iannis is introduced as central character, and history and miracles as central themes.
2 Mussolini is ridiculed and the historical context is established.
3 Villagers are introduced and Pelagia and Mandras are brought together.
4 Carlo in Albania is preparing to invade Greece.
5 Metaxas, Greek Prime Minister and dictator, reviews the situation.
6 Carlo in Albania falls in love with Francesco.
7 Father Arsenios has a problem; Dr Iannis takes pity on him.
8 Lemoni finds Psipsina; Mandras' courtship of Pelagia begins.

Chapters 9–14: Pelagia's relationship with Mandras against a backdrop of impending war

9 15 August 1940: the Italians provoke the Greeks by sinking the Elli at Tinos.
10 Carlo and Francesco are sent to trigger war by killing fellow Italians.
11 Pelagia and Mandras become closer, but Dr Iannis has denied Pelagia a dowry.
12 On the Feast Day of St Gerasimos, a drunken Mandras proposes to Pelagia.
13 Pelagia secretly spies on Mandras swimming naked with dolphins; he announces he is going to Albania to fight.
14 Metaxas rejects Mussolini's ultimatum; war commences between Italy and Greece.

Chapters 15–22: the Albanian campaign for the Greeks and the Italians; the tragic perspective

15 Carlo and Francesco suffer terribly during the invasion of Greece.
16 Letters from Pelagia to Mandras at the front.
17 In Albania the war worsens in atrociously icy conditions.
18 Dr Iannis tries to write a chapter of his History, again eaten by the goat (as in ch. 1).
19 Carlo reports Francesco's death, contrasting the sanitised official version with the appalling truth.

Chapters 23–27: the arrival of Corelli with the Italian occupying forces, and initial hostilities

Chapters 28–36: Weber, ELAS, and the growing love affair

Chapters 37–42: passion and music

Chapters 43–49: premonitions of tragedy; threatened Arcadia

43 A mine is detonated on the beach with spectacular and fatal consequences.

44 Corelli punishes two Italian soldiers who stole chickens from Kokolios.

45 Pelagia and Corelli drive around the island on a motorcycle and stay at Casa Nostra.

46 Bunny Warren, British SOE officer, parachutes onto Mount Aenos and baffles Alekos.

47 Dr Iannis warns Pelagia of the likely conseqences of her love for Corelli.

48 La Scala meets at Dr Iannis' house; Weber's racist views are attacked.

49 Dr Iannis warns Corelli of the likely conseqences of his love for Pelagia.

Chapters 50–61: crisis and massacre; Corelli's departure

50 Summary of small military engagements in the Aegean in this period (1943).

51 Mussolini is sacked; Italy changes sides; the Italians on Cephallonia are endangered.

52 The crisis develops; Hitler orders the murder of all Italian soldiers on Cephallonia.

53 The battery of Captain Appollonio opens fire on the Germans, and Corelli approves.

54 Carlo's farewell letter anticipates his death.

55 The Germans begin to kill the Italian soldiers systematically.

56 Weber is responsible for executing the men of La Scala; Carlo saves Corelli's life by standing in front of him.

57 Velisarios finds Corelli; Arsenios is shot witnessing the burning of Italian bodies.

58 Velisarios brings Corelli, and Carlo's body, to Dr Iannis and Pelagia.

59 Dr Iannis and Pelagia heal Corelli using mandolin strings and hide him in the cachette.

60 Corelli is moved to Casa Nostra; Bunnios agrees to evacuate him.

61 Pelagia says farewell to Corelli as he sets off in a caïque for Sicily.

Chapters 62–67: war and peace; earthquake; the next generation

62 The Germans vandalise Cephallonia and depart; Psipsina is killed. Weber leaves his gramophone to Pelagia, as promised.

63 ELAS members emerge from hiding, abduct the doctor, and kill Bunnios; Mandras assaults Pelagia, is disowned by Drosoula and drowns himself.

Pelagia and Drosoula adopt an abandoned baby, Antonia; the abducted Dr Iannis returns, but is now dumb. Corelli returns for the first time, and misinterprets the baby in Pelagia's arms.

65 The earthquake: Dr Iannis is killed and the house is destroyed.

66 The international rescue effort for Cephallonia includes an Italian fireman, Corelli.

67 Pelagia laments her fate: the loss of two beloved men.

Chapters 68–73: a fourth generation, and the reunion

68 Pelagia decides to complete her father's history of Cephallonia.

69 Antonia marries Alexi and has a son, Iannis; Drosoula opens a taverna; she later dies.

70 Velisarios opens the cachette; Iannis is taught to play bouzouki and mandolin.

71 Iannis learns to play Corelli's mandolin and comforts Pelagia.

72 October 1993; an old man finds Iannis playing Antonia, his mandolin.

73 Pelagia and Corelli, reunited, relive the past; they tour the island and visit Casa Nostra on a motorcycle.

Timeline

Political/historical events	Personal/community events
1940	
August The *Elli* is sunk	**August** Dr Iannis starts his History; Pelagia is 17; Velisarios injures Mandras and carries him to doctor; Mandras falls in love with Pelagia; Lemoni finds Psipsina
October Metaxas refuses Italian ultimatum; Julia Division in Albania including Carlo and Francesco; Francesco dies	**October** Mandras proposes to Pelagia; Mandras goes to war on Greek/Albanian border
1941	
	Spring Mandras returns, horribly changed
April Acqui Division occupies Cephallonia	**April** Corelli billeted on Dr Iannis and Pelagia
ELAS operations in the Peloponnese	Mandras is recruited by ELAS in Peloponnese; Corelli meets Weber; anonymous Anti-Fascist pamphlet distributed; 'Pelagia's March' composed; snail-hunting; lovers enjoy motorcycle and Casa Nostra; mine is inexpertly detonated

1943	September		September
	Overthrow of Mussolini; vacillation of General Gandin on Cephallonia; Weber ordered to massacre his La Scala friends; thousands of Italian bodies burned		Corelli decides to resist German attack; Carlo saves Corelli; Velisarios carries him to doctor; the doctor and Pelagia dress his wounds; Carlo is buried under the olive tree; Arsenios is killed and burned by the Germans; Corelli convalesces in cachette and Casa Nostra; Corelli leaves island with aid of Bunny Warren

1944	November		November
	Germans leave Cephallonia		Psipsina killed by Germans as they leave; partisans kill Warren and abduct doctor, Stamatis and Kokolios to mainland where latter two die; Mandras, now literate, returns again in December and attempts to rape Pelagia who shoots him. Drosoula disowns Mandras who drowns himself; baby found and named Antonia

1946		Doctor returns but will not speak
		October Pelagia sees 'ghost' of Corelli

1953	August		Doctor is killed in earthquake; house destroyed
	The earthquake		
			Pelagia completes her father's History; Antonia marries Alexi and has child Iannis; Velisarios opens cachette and mandolin is found
1993			**October** Corelli identifies himself to Iannis and is reunited with Pelagia

Chapter notes

1 The novel starts with a miracle (word used in first paragraph), the establishment of the importance of restitution and healing, and the impossibility of recording a true history. To create humour and identify the doctor as an intelligent character distinct from the average villager, the diction is incongruously technical and sophisticated. The huge number of classical references in this chapter indicate the parallel story of Odysseus running through the novel and the comparisons to be made between mortal and immortal heroes. A goat features in this opening chapter and reappears as a symbol in the final chapter of the novel.

2 This dramatic monologue, fantasy but based on historical fact, satirises Mussolini's megalomania and vanity and ironically exposes him to self-generated ridicule. Like Dr Iannis, he has a daughter. It introduces the reader to a big man who will have a devastating effect on the lives of little men, and the ironies

inherent in these terms, especially given that Mussolini was a notoriously small man in physical stature. His cat phobia can be contrasted to the way other, better, characters treat cats, and suggests that Mussolini dislikes their independence.

'**Vogliamo la pace e non vogliamo la guerra**': 'We want peace and we don't want war' — not an acceptable statement for fascists.

'**Church, kitchen and children**': a slogan of Nazi Germany pertaining to the role of women.

Tellini incident of 1923: an Italian officer was killed on the Greek–Albanian border. The Italians blamed the Greek government and bombarded and invaded Corfu; the League of Nations made Mussolini withdraw.

Tsamouria: a region of northwestern Greece inhabited predominantly by Albanians.

Epirus: a disputed region between Greece and Albania.

3 Alekos will be the same at the end of the novel as at the beginning; he represents the 'slow endurance' of the island through time and the lofty Olympian view of the doings of the little people from the mountain heights. In this chapter is the first of many explosions, and the treatment of serious as comic in the way the injury of Mandras is described; the love affair between him and Pelagia has been determined by Velisarios in his role as the strongman of fate.

'**the incarceration of Jews and homosexuals, gypsies and the mentally afflicted**': all of these groups of people were imprisoned and many of them exterminated in Nazi Germany.

Guernica and Abyssinia: Guernica, a town in northern Spain, was devastated by aerial bombing during the Spanish Civil War, an event immortalised by Picasso in the painting of the same name; in Abyssinia the Italians used poison gas in a war with the Abyssinian people.

Darwin: Charles Darwin's theory of evolution was abused by Nazis to justify their belief that the Germans (Aryans) were a superior race, and occasioned their interest in 'eugenics' — systematic breeding of superior human specimens.

Ionia: Cephallonia is one of the Ionian islands, but they are not known as Ionia, because that is an area of Asia Minor, since 1923 part of Turkey.

4 Carlo is another Atlas figure, the strong man on the opposing side, whose Platonic homosexuality further links him to ancient Greece, as well as to the Christian ideal of being prepared to lay down one's life for one's brother. He neatly combines the novel's two strands of love and war, and his testament, which will not be read until he is dead, is a historical document.

Casa Rosetta: literally the Rose House; a brothel.

Plato: for the ancient Athenians homosexuality was a noble expression of human love. The ideal of a homosexual band of soldiers actually existed in the Sacred band of Thebes, all 300 of whose warriors were found dead in a circle after the battle of Chaironea.

alchemy: throughout the Middle Ages it was believed that through alchemy (a forerunner of chemistry) base metals could be transformed into gold by the 'elixir'.

5 This is a sympathetic portrait of the dying Greek dictator General Metaxas, also worried about his wayward daughter, which intertwines the personal and the political. It suggests that even dictators are sometimes motivated by an attempt to make the honourable decision, even if this is not the way uncharitable official history records them, and that they are, like little men, at the mercy of fate and subject to the 'requirements of classical tragedy'. Unlike Mussolini, Metaxas can perceive that perhaps he has been nothing but 'an absurd little man'. He states that 'Everything ends in death', but this view will be contradicted by other characters and elements in the novel, and by his own legendary status for rejecting the Italian ultimatum on 28 October 1940. The battle of Thermopylae is an example of a historical miracle, since Leonidas and a force of 300 Spartans held off the invading Persians for 2 days until a traitor showed the invaders a way to outflank the defenders.

National Youth Organisation: Metaxas was a neo-fascist and, like all fascist dictators, founded a youth organisation to give military training and instil nationalism.
Übermensch: higher man, the goal of Nazi eugenic programmes.

6 Carlo blames fate for his sexual orientation. He makes important comments about history and tragedy, and conveys political information about the Albanian campaign as well as lyrical personal reflections on his beloved Francesco. He introduces the concepts of martyrdom and forgiveness.

Alpini: Italian mountain troops.
Jonathan and David: celebrated pair of homosexual lovers in the Bible.
Bersaglieri: snipers, élite troops.
Mare Nostrum: Our Sea, a Roman phrase, used by Mussolini to remind people of Italy's commanding position in the centre of the Mediterranean.

7 In contrast to the poignant previous chapter of Carlo's testament, this is bathos and farce of the crudest kind. It suggests the ambivalent position of the church in the community, whereby a priest is both respected and ridiculed as a representative of the divine who suffers acutely from human failings. As so often, the doctor takes pity on and cures him while Velisarios does the carrying of the 'body' to the doctor's house.

venturi effect: acceleration of fluid in a narrowing tube; named after Italian scientist Venturi.

Machian variety of materialism: Ernst Mach (1838–1916) was an Austrian positivist philosopher.

Hippocratic oath: oath taken by all doctors, based on Hippocrates, ancient Greek physician.

8 Cats, which include pine martens, girls and 'pussycats' (whores) — all vulnerable and victimised — are a recurring feature of the novel. They not only create humour but are a touchstone for the humanity of the characters who come into contact with them. Psipsina caught on the wire is a metaphor for the destructiveness of war and what will happen to the Italians later. Dr Iannis' surgical skills are miraculous, because they are performed with faith and love. Pelagia accuses Mandras of being even madder than her father. Lemoni brings the child's-eye view into the equation.

the Orsini family: Giovanni Orsini acquired Cephallonia in the twelfth century as part of his wife's dowry.

'King Alexander died of a monkey bite': Alexander died on 25 October 1920 following a bite from a pet monkey.

hachoir: a small axe (French).

9 Perceptions change under pressure, and the royalist and the communist can be united in solidarity by a threat to something greater than political allegiances: the homeland, a version of Casa Nostra. The doctor's refusal to offer Mandras a dowry triggers the latter's need to prove himself a hero and reflects the clash between traditional and modern attitudes to women. Many of the public events in the novel take place in August, and this attack on the Virgin's feast day on 15 August is sacrilege. This chapter is an example of the sudden mood changes which typify the novel.

nargiles: a hookah (communal pipe).

Venizelist: supporter of Eleftherios Venizelos (qv); a liberal.

Feast of the Dormition of the Virgin Mary: 15 August.

'howl ye ships of Tarshish': Isaiah 23.

10 Such staged incidents were common at this time; on the eve of the Second World War, German soldiers dressed as Poles 'attacked' German territory to justify Hitler's invasion of Poland. This is a complicating factor for history.

'Francesco and I were saved by the weather' is another example of the intervention of fate, and the irony of the doomed soldiers becoming unintentional heroes shows the absurdity and arbitrariness of war.

catharsis: literally 'cleaning', more figuratively a cleansing of the soul.

11 In these streams of consciousness by Mandras and Pelagia, giving the very different male and female perspectives and daily lives of this time, the lyrical/poetic and domestic/prosaic are juxtaposed. Homeric dolphins and living ghosts both make a preview appearance. There are hints that the relationship will not have a happy outcome: Pelagia is already 'a bit sick of fish' and we realise that the doctor does not consider Mandras a suitable husband for her.

clouts: rags (strips of cloth for use as sanitary towels).
'there's never any luck on a Tuesday': because Constantinople fell to the Turks on a Tuesday in 1453, there is a Greek superstition that Tuesday is an unlucky day, particularly among fishermen.
Ithaca and Zante and Levkas: these are the three neighbouring Ionian islands, suggesting that Mandras has never been as far as the mainland. Zante is the old Italian name for Zakynthos.

12 October is the month of miracles and anniversaries in the novel. The patron saint of Cephallonia, Gerasimos, is a ghostly presence, similar to his human parallel Alekos, who gets involved when events are particularly worrying. Two miracles are needed this year. The carnival festival in this chapter wears the classical drama mask of comedy — feasting, dancing, social harmony — and is a Bacchic ritual ironically juxtaposed with the tragedy to follow. Love and war arrive together, as kinds of madness.

accidental shooting of Procris: see p. 19 above.
St Gerasimos: patron saint of Cephallonia. Born in 1507 at Trikala on the mainland, he lived for 12 years in the Holy Land prior to settling on Cephallonia and setting up a nunnery at Omala. He dedicated his life to good works on behalf of the villagers, dying in 1579. Miracles soon followed, and when his body was exhumed 2 years later it had not decomposed, so he was declared a saint. His feast days are 16 August (the anniversary of his death) and 20 October (the date of his exhumation).
opiate of the masses: Karl Marx dismissed religion in this phrase.

13 There are several ominous clues about 'adamantine' Mandras and his future in this chapter. It is suggested that there are two kinds of Greek (see ch. 49), and that Pelagia 'would only ever be able to marry happily with a foreigner'. Mandras is linked with a rifle, and will be associated with guns throughout the novel. He plays the role of a beautiful Greek god, in this reversal of the mythological Venus and Adonis bathing scene, which will make his physical transformation in the Albanian campaign all the more shocking. The three dolphins are the first of several symbolic groups of three in the novel; three is a literary and mystical number deriving from biblical, mythological and folkloric sources. The last word of this chapter about Mandras is, prophetically, 'death'.

gibbous moon: between half and full moon; associated with death and horror.
adamantine: diamond hard (cf. the use of ice as a symbol; 'Ice in the soul' as recommended by Mussolini in ch. 2; Mandras as 'the Wild Man of the Ice' in ch. 20).
derringer: a very small pistol.
the Internationale: the anthem of communists worldwide.
Nereid: sea-nymph.
Potamid: river-nymph (the word appears to be a coining by the author).
Tsamoria: variant of Tsamouria (ch. 2).

14 Grazzi is another pawn who, like Günter Weber, is led by fate into playing a dishonourable part in events that 'will cause history to heap him with opprobrium and contempt'. The concept of honour, which is the only guarantee of being remembered well, is crucial to the reader's judgement of characters and events, and the way history is judged.

Ala Littoria: Italian airline (literally, Wings of the Coast).
Palazzo Chigi: the Italian Foreign Ministry.
Stefani Agency: Italian news agency.
Madama Butterfly: opera by Puccini about a tragic love affair between a serviceman and an islander in which the foreigner does not keep his promise to return and marry his betrothed.
Kifisia: an attractive suburb to the north of Athens.

15 Carlo gives evidence of the 'acts of lunacy' committed in wartime. He introduces Corelli here for the first time, linking him to Francesco. The horrors of fighting in ice, representing inhumanity, are graphically portrayed.

irredentists: those who seek to regain land which once belonged to a country. Mussolini used the phrase '*Italia Irredenta*' (literally, unredeemed Italy) to refer to territory he wished to conquer.
Golgotha: literally, the place of skulls; the hill outside Jerusalem where Christ was crucified.

16 Pelagia's letters, full of local and war news, become shorter and increasingly despondent as she receives no reply during autumn and winter and the period of Lent comes upon the community. She ends by telling Mandras that she feels fate is against the bedcover she has been attempting to make.

feston and fil-tiré: embroidery techniques.

17 Francesco, an animal-lover, goes mad. Pathos is created by Francesco's farewell letter to his mother, which prefigures Carlo's to Corelli. Letters are not only historical documents but links between past, present and future in the novel.

SM79s: the Savoia-Marchetti SM.79 was the best bomber in the Italian Air Force.

18 There are several references to Homer and Odysseus in this chapter, which is a wide-ranging mixture of private musings and historical commentary. Prophetically, the doctor refers to the 'Italian Occupation' of the Venetians. The goat's diet obliquely comments on the strange fate and complete absence of many historical documents.

Muslim...Koran...Hafiz: a Muslim is a follower of the religion of Islam. The Koran is the Holy Book of Islam. A Hafiz is one who has memorised all the Koran.
the Dodecanese: 12 islands in the Aegean near the coast of Turkey — the most easterly of the Greek islands. They were granted to Italy by the Treaty of Sèvres after the First World War.
the Italian occupation: see pp. 13–14.

19 The disparity between truth and fiction is ironic and moving, and draws attention once again to the impossibility of memories and records of historical events being accurate (especially in wartime, when euphemisms are used to make horrific death more palatable to grief-stricken loved ones) and to the huge divergence between points of view even of those who share an experience. Francesco dies in an explosion, one of many fire images in the novel.

20 Mandras returns in March 1941, and though he has only been away for a few months, he is transformed and his 'homecoming' is far from being a happy event. Like Odysseus, he is not recognised by his loved ones, only by an animal. The chapter title and his appearance suggest that Mandras has become a mythical monster — the product of war.

21 Drosoula's family history (which is the subject of de Bernières' prequel to Captain Corelli, *Birds Without Wings*) is a tormented one which nevertheless has made her strong and self-sufficient. She is an ugly, single woman in a society which values beauty and is suspicious of a woman without a mate. Once again Mandras requires treatment in the doctor's house, but this time Pelagia takes on the mantle of the expert and blooms with 'a sudden sense of vocation' in a scene reminiscent of Christ's body being laid out by women. In several respects Mandras is a Christian martyr and disciple — an illiterate fisherman — as well as being an Odysscus figure.

Lausanne settlement: treaty of 1923 settling the dispute between Greece and Turkey. The surviving Greek population of Smyrna and Asia Minor was moved to Greece in an early form of 'ethnic cleansing'.
Pontos accent: Greeks from Asia Minor are still known as 'Pontians' and have a distinctive accent.

22 In his account of his return from the horrific experiences in the Albanian mountains, Mandras prophetically mentions the figure of Death which has cut

him off from the people at home. This is one of many changes of perception and values in the novel. His odyssey contains direct parallels to that of his literary ancestor and includes Pelagia as the chaste Penelope, the threatening females of Scylla and Charybdis and the Cyclopean Circe. He describes an epiphanic moment when he realised that there is a 'madness…in the very manufacture of the world', and a miraculous vision of the angel Gabriel (for which there are documented accounts during the First World War). Mandras has obviously suffered mental as well as physical degeneration, and is a victim of fanaticism and despair in that he wants to go back as soon as he is able.

Stukas: German dive-bombers. They created terror with their banshee-like wail as they dived towards their target.

23 The chapter starts with a ghost story, which will become an increasingly common feature in the novel. Approaching war — Corfu has already fallen — causes changes of allegiance and a questioning of beliefs. The kitchen cavity is mentioned, which is suggestive of a grave and which will become a time capsule. Mandras, like Odysseus, and for inscrutable reasons, retreats into feigned and inconsistent states of madness and loses Pelagia's sympathy. The feast of the resurrection — a theme in the novel — is ironically counterpointed by Mandras' physical rising from his bed but mental decline into brutality. His treatment of Pelagia is further juxtaposed with the arrival of Corelli, with his instrumental other half, and his chivalrous salutation to a 'bella bambina'. Mood changes occur several times in this chapter.

Kathimerini: Athens newspaper.

24 Carlo confirms that the experience of Albania and the death of Francesco have changed his romantic attitude to war. He describes Corelli as a kind of saint, which is how Pelagia has previously described her father because of his gift for healing. He admits some people think Corelli 'a little mad'. Corelli's practical jokes include the subversive parodying of a military memo.

Arcadia: an idealised pastoral landscape, but also an area of the Peloponnese in Greece.

25 The first meeting between the doctor, Pelagia and Corelli is unexpectedly comic, partly thanks to Psipsina. The novel continues to subvert reader expectations of sentimental moments. Corelli has haemorrhoids, not at all an attribute of the stereotypical romantic lover. The defacing of the statue (the Italians 'chipped away the letters') is an attempt to erase history.

'Mea culpa…': 'I have sinned…' — the normal opening of a Catholic confession.

'To The Glory Of The British People': a reminder of the period when the island was a British protectorate.

26 Corelli's dream of 'dolphins with sharp edges' suggests the dangerousness of Mandras and the deterioration of his relationship with Pelagia, as also symbolised by the waistcoat which 'doesn't quite match up' because the two sides have a slightly different pattern. Corelli's association with children and animals is established, and the power of creative art to bring like-minded people together.

Peloponnisos: the Peloponnese, the Greek mainland adjacent to Cephallonia.

27 Animals and music bring the two destined lovers together. Pelagia has an epiphany when she realises that music is 'an emotional and intellectual odyssey'. This clichéd romantic interlude is undermined by the doctor turning it into a comedy.

purfled: see p. 22.

28 The first of several ironic titles, this is a reference to Marxist ideology. It is the beginning of a sustained attack on ELAS and the British who allowed them to operate. Mandras is now only an ironic representation of Odysseus the wanderer as he falls prey to Hector's ideology of 'historical necessity', imagines that he can become a god through violence, and enjoys having power over the old man and his daughter, who remind him of the doctor and Pelagia. This is one of the most shocking incidents in the novel, and shows what humans can descend to in the name of politics when they lose touch with the personal. Weber will follow the same decline.

Roumeli: the area of mainland Greece north of the Peloponnese.
ELAS/EAM/KKE/EDES: see pp. 14–15.

29 This chapter is in a very different mood from the previous one, and juxtaposed for maximum contrast. Notice the ubiquitous little girl at the end of the chapter, who symbolises the vulnerable innocence of Greece.

30 The ironic, possibly oxymoronic, title expresses the view, through the introduction of Günter Weber, that it is ideologies which damage natural humanity. Though a virgin, he has become as much a whore in his uniform as the 'pussycats' who provide their services to the Italian army. He is 'destined to betray with a Judas kiss' as a pawn in a game he doesn't understand. Significantly, he 'could not sing a note'.

31 Pelagia's washing of Corelli's gun is treated comically, but could easily have taken a different turn. As elsewhere, love and guns are juxtaposed, and this incident serves the purpose of bringing out their suppressed feelings for one another and moving the relationship into the next stage of physical contact, childlike behaviour and musical inspiration.

32 The degree to which Mandras has been brainwashed is apparent in his worship of Comrade Hector, Homer's brave prince and warrior of Troy. Had Mandras not been illiterate he would not have been so impressed by political tags and Hector's ability to read Lenin, or so grateful for his promise to teach him to read. History achieves its effects by offering disaffected individuals a chance to be accepted and to feel a sense of belonging in an organisation. The title is ironic in that it is the peasants' property which is being 'liberated', and Mandras' mind which has been captivated.

'They blew a bridge yesterday': blowing up the Gorgopotamos viaduct was the greatest achievement of the andartes against the Germans (see p. 14 above).

33 Hands are the next stage after eye contact. Pelagia's blanket is not only not growing; it is 'ever diminishing', like her interest in her fiancé. This scene of Corelli's physical embarrassment is typical de Bernières — bawdy and similar to that of Arsenios and the wine bottles. It causes Corelli to become an affectionate domestic animal, a far cry from the conventional literary hero and brave soldier.

34 The British do not come out well in this scene between Myers and Hector, as they continue to supply ELAS even though they understand its devious practices. But this is a matter of self-interest and expediency, the first principles of politics, which cause the wrong people to rise to the top. The British are caricatured by their stereotypical language of 'ripping', 'top-hole' and 'cup of tea'.

Liberator: the name of an American bomber used for this purpose, but ironic in view of the chapter title.
Glücksburg: when Greece became independent they needed a king, and invited a member of the German House of Glücksburg to take up the post; a cynical way of referring to the king.

35 In parody of a propaganda pamphlet, this chapter pretends to idolise 'The Madman' and refers to Him in capitals as a divine being, while simultaneously revealing some discreditable facts about Him, most of which are true, and satirising the dictator for His vanity, inconstancy and stupidity. The tone changes when irony is replaced by denunciation halfway through. It is an interesting point for debate whether 'every nation gets the leaders it deserves'.

Giovinezza: the fascist anthem.

36 With another ironic title, this chapter shows how Mandras and others like him are brainwashed with jargon into voting for things they don't understand by people whom they mistake for saints. They are victims of their own ignorance and of superior power cynically wielded, and there have been many of them in the course of history. On the other hand, perhaps history cannot ever be distinguished from propaganda.

37 Pelagia's reaction is a comment on the difficulty of distinguishing between heroism and madness.

38 The origins of the march are a combination of Corelli's hangover, Pelagia's kindnesses and anger, love and war. Creativity is personal and spontaneous, unlike destruction.

39 Father Arsenios is paradoxically 'saved by the war'; given a mission, he now becomes the saintly opposite of his self-indulgent former self, a Cassandra-like prophet preaching doom and judgement, fated to be disbelieved, in a language which is a mixture of biblical imagery and local place names.

40 The penultimate stage of the growing rapprochement of the would-be lovers takes place as an alleged 'mistake' whereby Corelli significantly substitutes for the doctor, whom he resembles in character if not in body, as the recipient of Pelagia's kiss.

41 The moment of coming together is symbolised by snails and treated light-heartedly in this chapter. However, the situation is a traditional romantic one in which a chivalrous male rescues a trapped female when Pelagia, like Psipsina previously, and in the same place, gets ensnared. This time love rather than war is suggested by the image. There is a sudden tone change to sentimental at the end.

42 This is the only time in the novel we have a stream of lyrical consciousness from Corelli, now a man in love who can see many similarities between Antonia and Pelagia, the two women in his life. He appreciates the paradox that the war brought them together and will also prise them apart.

43 Lemoni's language, 'The Great Big Spiky Rustball', entitles the chapter, which tells of Corelli's childish delight in explosions and the lover's desire to show off, and shows how nearly comedy and tragedy are allied. Once again, Carlo has to carry an injured loved one.

44 Though this chapter begins in comic vein, it ends with the heartbreaking loss of Pelagia's goat, and a debt to be repaid.

45 Note that Corelli and Pelagia became lovers only in 'the old-fashioned sense'. It distorts the novel to imagine that Pelagia is not still a virgin when she is recovered half a century later, when she is owed a life. This is an unconsummated love affair, and likely to remain so. The motorbike is an alternative 'musical machine' to the mandolin. This is an idyllic pastoral chapter — Eden before evil entered.

46 Bunnios is introduced as a British caricature called 'it'. Speaking the equivalent of Chaucerian English and wearing antique clothing, he provides a historic as well as a comic dimension. He also has a miraculous radio. The top of Mt Aenos is a world beyond time and humans.

SOE: Special Operations Executive, responsible for supporting resistance organisations in occupied European countries.

47 The unenviable position of women as the repository of family honour is stressed by the doctor's warning to his daughter not to give in to the physical demands of the 'mad' captain, the angel with haemorrhoids. This chapter contains a movingly lyrical passage describing married love.

48 The different temperaments of the German and the Italian are exposed here, but Weber is not simply a stereotypical Nazi: he appreciates music and is prepared to discuss ethical issues 'amiably' with the Italians in Italian.

49 The description of 'the two Greeks inside every Greek' is relevant to their presentation as a nationality in the novel. The character of Homer's 'wily Odysseus' is composed of a synthesis of the 'Hellene' and the 'Romoi'.

sophrosune: usually sophrosyne; the Platonic ideal of temperance, moderation, prudence and self-restraint.

50 There is a list of alleged miracles at the start of the chapter; war engenders myths.

limber: wagon or truck carrying ammunition.
breach: should be 'breech' — part of a field gun.

51 The 'apocalyptic heat of August' is preparation for an explosion. Corelli has become Greek in his nostalgia for a place about to be lost, Cephallonia.

52 To suggest time speeding up and the lack of control of the participants in history, this chapter mixes short passages in a variety of voices and genres, juxtaposing the big men and the little men, the Italian disarray with the German treachery, ending with the British expediency.

panzers: German tanks.
Luftwaffe: German Air Force.
Junkers: German bombers.
francs-tireurs: irregular soldiers.

53 One can never know the motivation for amazing acts, and therefore history itself is impossible. The battle of Argostoli is a scene from Armageddon, and a preview of others to come, including the earthquake.

54 This poignant and prophetic letter speaks 'from beyond the grave', calling attention to the time paradox inherent in writing in the present about the past in a form which will only be discovered in the future, the new present, and which will alter the view of the past. Memory is a key concept in the novel, as we are reminded by Carlo's Hamlet-like last instruction.

55 Can there be victory in war, and who is claiming it? There is military and moral victory — not the same thing. Alekos, above it all, finds the battle beautiful. Pelagia shifts her priorities from the political to the personal: 'Who cares about Greece? Where is Antonio?' Corelli experiences a shift of perception: the crushed head of a little girl (Psipsina's fate) makes him resolve that the war must be taken seriously and won. His farewell to Pelagia is moving and honourable.

56 Weber is the unwilling instrument of fate that 'had called him to the killing of his friends'; the magnanimous Corelli, singing his way to death, forgives him. The massacre is not presented in a sentimental way, but is the more poignant for that. Both Carlo and Weber play a part in saving Corelli, though with very different motivations and consequences for themselves. The reader is privileged to know their thinking, which the participants do not know and cannot guess.

57 The Day of Judgement and Armageddon have come to Cephallonia, with fire and burning bodies. Alekos, from his immortal perspective, thinks it may be 'the end of the world'. The evidence for 'historical truth' is being deliberately destroyed. The nationalities merge as the Greek priest shares the fate of the Italian soldiers. St Gerasimos is reputed to have been conjured from his grave by these atrocities.

Armageddon: the site of the Last Battle on Judgement Day (Mount Megiddo in Palestine); now interchangeably used for the place or the event.

58 Once again, a strong man carries an injured body to be resurrected by the doctor, the hardest miracle yet. Carlo is buried in 'the soil of Odysseus' time' like a god of the ancient world who 'had belonged there from the first'. His funeral mythologises him, and is associated with imagery of the renewal of nature. Afterwards 'the first birds sang'.

59 The miracle of Corelli's survival, suggesting a hopeful outcome for Europe ultimately, is due to the strings of the mandolin, which symbolise the human spirit. During his time in the hideaway Corelli becomes even more Greek by growing a beard. His first solid meal is snails. He has been saved and resurrected by the love of five people, including, ironically, Weber.

60 Pelagia prepares to take on the role of Penelope, abandoned and faithfully awaiting her lover's return from the sea.

'Semper fidelis': 'always faithful' (Latin).

61 The title of this chapter echoes George Eliot in *Scenes of Clerical Life*: 'In every parting there is an image of death'. The doctor recognises that Corelli has 'become an islander, like us', and prophesies a return he will not live to see. He goes off to help a doomed little girl. Corelli experiences again a moment of homesickness as he leaves Cephallonia 'like a ghost'.

Standard SOPs: SOPs are Standard Operational Practices, so the additional 'standard' is redundant.

62 A change of perception occurs when a new horror makes a previous one seem less bad; the Italians are no longer the enemies of the Greeks. Rape can be political as well as personal: Cephallonia is pillaged by 'automata without principles'.

'Mein Ruh ist hin...': lines from Goethe's *Faust*: 'My peace is gone, my heart is heavy, I will never find you again...'

63 This passage is a strong indictment in uncompromising language ('hooligans') of the communist partisans in mainland Greece and is the cause of contention between Greeks and the author. At this lowest point in her life, everything else having been taken from her, Pelagia finds the love of a mother in Drosoula, whose 'spirit was unbroken'. And the symbolic bedcover 'miraculously' grows. In a repeat scenario, Mandras arrives unannounced and unrecognised, and to put Pelagia through a 'torment identical to that which she had suffered so many months before'. This time it is even worse, however, because he has learned to read. The reader's response to Mandras in this chapter is complex: he is a killer and a rapist, but he is also a victim, a god turned animal, grief-stricken and banished from the embrace of home, lover and mother. His death is a 'liberation', purification and a return to the sea of the innocent youth who played and loved and hoped. The three dolphins turn him into a myth.

64 A product of rape can be new life. The female baby, abandoned in fairy-tale fashion, is an act of fate, a reincarnation of Corelli and his mandolin, a next generation for a family which would otherwise have died out, a consolation for the broken doctor, and the forming of a female trio. Her life-long adoption of white clothes presumably suggests her affinity to angels and goddesses. A new cat shares with her the recycled name of Psipsina. (Cats have returned to the island from apparent extinction.) In another resurrection, in the month of anniversaries, the 'ghost' of Corelli appears, in the same spot that Mandras first appeared in the novel, bringing peace to Pelagia — and frustration to the reader.

the barbarians: the reference is to the celebrated poem 'Waiting for the Barbarians' by the Greek poet Constantine Cavafis.
lugubrious Canadian poet: this fictional character has strong similarities to Leonard Cohen, who settled in such a house on the Greek island of Hydra.

65 Pelagia becomes Italian in spirit in contempt for Greeks and to feel closer to Corelli. In August, the month of explosions, the earthquake occurs like the fury of the gods. The silenced Dr Iannis finds dying words which characteristically express a desire to save others as his home collapses on him.

Romaic Greek: Greek as spoken by the refugees who left Asia Minor in 1923.

66 Velisarios comes back to life as a tower of strength and resurrects the village physically and spiritually. In a moment of miraculous coincidence, but which is perfectly possible, the fireman Corelli sees Carlo in his grave, suggesting that the past is never really past. Carlo is then reburied, showing that even a funeral can repeat itself.

67 With a title suggestive of a piece of music, to contrast with 'Pelagia's March', this chapter is an elegy in the first person for all that Pelagia, reduced to being her 'own ghost', has lost, and for her beloved father in particular. This contrasts with the previous chapter in stressing the transience and ephemerality of life, and the permanence of loss.

68 The Cephallonians were changed by the earthquake. Pelagia's 'madness' of grief is cured by Antonia's pretend dream of the ghost of the doctor asking for Pelagia to continue his History. 'Pelagia almost became the doctor', writing from memory with his spiritual guidance. She concludes that humans are fundamentally insane, and that freedom and order are two sides of the same coin.

69 Whimsical ghostly postcards provide another linguistic dimension to the novel. The union of Alexi and Antonia, at the age Pelagia was at the start of the novel, is not a typical story-book romance. Pelagia takes on her father's role of taverna story-teller and local character. Politics is still a strong consideration in the life of Cephallonians in the 1970s, and they are still plagued by dictators. The name of Iannis is reallocated.

the Colonels: in 1967 there was a military coup mounted by 'the Colonels'.

70 Spiridon from Corfu, an exuberant virtuoso performer on the bouzouki who admits that the mandolin is the instrument of his heart, is obviously a reincarnation of Corelli. Pelagia's awakened desire for a time-machine to revisit the period of love in her life prefigures the novel's ending on the motorbike. Little Iannis' great grandfather has been mythologised into a doctor who 'could cure people just by touching them' (and 'Healer Of All Living Things' (ch. 68)). In several respects, including swinging on a branch of the olive tree and a fascination with guns, Iannis is Mandras returned. He and Spiro excavate history, as invested in places and objects, and summon the appearance of giant Velisarios, still miraculously able to perform a great feat of strength.

71 Alexi has undergone a complete change of perception and politics as a result of becoming a father. Pelagia relives her history through the photograph album and passes it down orally through the generations. She tells the boy who doesn't understand 'a present that had gone' that 'You die, and then someone comes to take your place'. We are given a preview of Iannis falling in love at the significant age of 17, using Corelli's mandolin.

72 Corelli is conjured by his mandolin, in the symbolic month of October, and his impulsive personality and use of language prove that some people don't change.

73 War and love demand restitution for debts owed. The reunion of the lovers is an unexpectedly comic scene. The olive branch of peace (and Homeric homecoming) is finally accepted. Corelli's perception of Carlo is changed by finally reading his papers, and he acknowledges that people are 'complicated'. Günter is described as 'grovelling and whining' in guilt when Corelli tracked him down. Corelli turned history into music, which ends with an 'unsatisfying conclusion that just faded away to silence'. Alekos restores the goat (called Restitution, symbolising the lost life) to Corelli and Pelagia, as a gift of the gods. The still mad Corelli acquires a motorbike and wears the 50-year-old waistcoat given to him instead of Mandras. Many of the other features of the novel are referred to in the final chapter, which looks backwards and forwards. The 'coquettish' Pelagia and the 'surprising' captain travel back in time to a second youth, which ends with a musical inspiration for 'the eternal spirit of Greece', and a mythological vision of three modern goddesses.

my Beatrice: the celebrated love of Dante for Beatrice is the basis of the *Divine Comedy.*
my Laura: the inspiration of Petrarch's Sonnets.
In both cases, the Italian writer fell for a young woman of great beauty who was unavailable, and the love was unrequited.

Characters

There are relatively few significant fictional characters in *Captain Corelli's Mandolin* and they repay careful study. It is a historical novel, in the sense that the fictional characters are placed squarely in a very specific and detailed historical context, and it is a distinctive feature of the book that these characters interact directly with authentic historical figures. Indeed, the author gives no indication when he is moving from one category to the other, and whilst most readers will know that Mussolini was fascist dictator of Italy during the Second World War, at one extreme, they are unlikely to know that Brigadier Myers or Captain Appollonio were also real people. The characters with whose development de Bernières is concerned are all fictional and most of them are listed below.

Major characters

Corelli

Given the title of the novel, Antonio Corelli must be treated as the main character, although he is not mentioned until ch. 15 and his first appearance is in ch. 23. He arrives with his mandolin and is inseparable from it before it actually becomes a physical part of him. His love for Pelagia can be seen as an extension of his love for his instrument; when he finally returns he finds the mandolin first, which leads him to the woman. His character is revealed in his love of singing, which represents his love of life, his sensitivity and how unsuited he is to being a soldier. Another important aspect of his character, and manifestation of his humanity, is his love of children and animals. His enjoyment of Psipsina and playfulness with Lemoni, and the affection he earns from both of them, are early indications of his tolerance and good nature. His naïvety about war and politics, his humour, exuberance, impulsiveness and liking for jokes all give him an aura of childlike innocence. He is a Romeo with piles, and therefore a real human creation rather than a conventional romantic hero, despite the fact that the Italian soldier with a mandolin was a stereotype in the interwar period. His creativity as a composer and the pleasure he provides as a musician are in direct and ironic contrast to the destructiveness of the war and the cynicism and philistinism of the 'great men', the leaders and decision-makers. Corelli plays the role of the little man with a big heart and gigantic courage, those who make a different kind of history, the one which really counts: the history of humanity. He chooses to be a lion, not a sheep; he 'remained a man of honour because he knew no other way to be' (p. 191). 'Why not smile in the face of death', he asks (p. 396), quoting the epigraph poem by Humbert Wolfe. He acknowledges the debt to someone who has made the supreme sacrifice, as shown by his annual pilgrimage to Carlo's grave. He can summon up 'intimations of Eden' (p. 440).

Pelagia

A beautiful Greek maiden, virgin, fairytale motherless child and romantic heroine with rival suitors, Pelagia is a victim of the times. She represents Cephallonia and Greece; she always smells of rosemary, which symbolises remembrance and fidelity in love. She is Drosoula's surrogate daughter and a reminder of his wife to Dr Iannis. She is a symbol of the ageing and suffering process, a repository of memories, an inspirer of music and a would-be Italian. She insists on putting the personal before the political and is 'too clever to be a humble wife'. She takes on her father's roles of writer and healer. Her sewing makes her an artist, and her art saves her lover's life.

Dr Iannis

Dr Iannis is a saint, a saviour, a healer, a writer and a humanist ('"You shouldn't trust to God for anything. These things are ours to ensure."' (p. 65)). Tolerant, with a sense of humour, he holds modern views on women and is a devoted father and grandfather. 'He thinks that he is a Socrates who can fly in the face of the custom' (p. 129); he is a martyr to the liberal cause. He understands love and history, and is a wise village patriarch whilst also being unconventional. He enjoys an argument and the loss of his voice is a symbol of free speech stamped out by oppression. His memory is overburdened with the horror of the darkness of war and the barbarianism of his fellow countrymen, but he remains an altruist to the end, never sacrifices his principles and after his death is mythologised.

Mandras

The novel presents Mandras as a Greek god, an Adonis/Poseidon figure, a fisher-man, and a disciple. He is a dolphin lover and an Odysseus-like traveller. He is illiterate and an unworthy suitor for Pelagia; he is by nature a soldier, not a lover. He becomes a communist by accident, and becomes the victim of indoctrina-tion and ignorance, representing the damage done by extreme politics. He has an 'adamantine' soul but suffers terribly in the ice. Mandras is a rejected son, a naïve youth who went astray and lost touch with personal values. A would-be rapist of Pelagia and Greece, and an actual murderer, he redeems his life by his death. He represents the two-sided nature of Greeks and is associated with the dictators Mussolini and Metaxas (ch. 13). He is the reverse of a fairytale prince in that he turned into a 'toad'; he 'lost his soul' to history and war. He became 'a shabby caricature of the man who had replaced him' (p. 447). He is associated with symmetry, 'a property of dead things' (p. 215). Though linked to Christ, he is a follower and not a leader, searching for an object of worship.

Secondary characters

Drosoula

A victim of the prejudice against widows, Drosoula illustrates the fate of the ugly woman. She has a previous history of suffering as a pawn of political expedience. She is a replacement mother for Pelagia and grandmother to Antonia, but is horrified by what her own son has become compared to what he might have been. She has an eye for business and is able to adapt; she is an independent survivor and represents the unbroken spirit of Greece. (De Bernières finds her a

sufficiently fascinating character to be writing a prequel to *Captain Corelli's Mandolin* based on her life before coming to Cephallonia.)

Carlo

The outsider: an individual, an intelligent observer, an animal lover, Carlo is a Homeric giant of body and heart, and represents the noble love between men in Plato's time. Hating barbarism, presented as a saviour and a martyr, he remains loyal to the death and becomes a posthumous hero who is given mythical status. His grave is a link with Homeric times and his burial is a symbol of the acceptance of the Italians by the Greek community; it is a site of pilgrimage for Corelli and Velisarios, and therefore the cause of a meeting between Velisarios and Iannis which results in the reunion of Corelli and Pelagia. He shows pity to Francesco and his mother; he introduces Corelli and shapes our attitude towards him. He is the anti-Judas figure who turns Weber's 30 pieces of silver into 30 seconds of sacrifice. In keeping his secret, he proves by his writings that people are not what they appear to be and that therefore history is impossible.

Weber

Weber is the oxymoronic 'Good Nazi', an inadequate would-be Aryan, a virgin trying to prove himself through a uniform and a doctrine, a racist and an animal-hater. His redeeming qualities are a love of music and being able to keep a promise to Pelagia, but he is weak in every situation, including his eventual hiding of his guilt in priesthood. He is, ironically and unwittingly, Corelli's saviour, and tries to get out of the order to massacre the Italians, but this is not recorded by the authorities. He has the grace, unlike the Croatian, to feel remorse, but he lacks the courage to refuse to carry out the death sentence (like Pontius Pilate). He attracts the reader's pity as well as contempt because de Bernières makes it clear he is a victim of fate in a terrible dilemma. He is a Judas, betrayed by history and destroyed by the war.

Symbolic characters

Arsenios represents the power of history to change people, and illustrates the position of the church in Greek village life. He has a devoted dog, in a novel which judges characters by their relationship with animals. He is a weak human who becomes a saint; he has the 'gift of prophecy' and is controlled by a kind of madness. Like Weber, 'he had no choice'. He is saved spiritually and destroyed physically by the war; he becomes a Christian martyr sharing a Homeric funeral pyre with the Italians he denounced but came to embrace through common suffering.

Lemoni represents the child's view and voice. She is an animal-saviour. She illustrates the love of children by humane characters, and vice versa. She is the pathos of war; there are many pseudo-Lemonis in the novel, i.e. references to suffering, dying or dead little girls made by Corelli and Dr Iannis.

Bunnios is a gentle satire of the British. A speaker of ancient Greek, he becomes a martyr of the civil war, and appears as an angel and a ghost. Like Corelli, he loves Greece and Greeks, and like Carlo, he risks his life for others.

Francesco is a man pushed beyond endurance. He shows his love for his mouse Mario. He is a victim of a hopeless war, a mad dictator, and ice. He is a precursor of Corelli as an Italian loved by Carlo.

Velisarios, the other giant, remains a strongman to the end and becomes a local legend. He brings about explosions and lovers' unions, and opens the historical cachette. He is an Atlas figure who bears human burdens.

Alekos is the good shepherd and a mountain spirit; he represents enduring and unchanging Greece, and takes an Olympian view of the war. A friend of Dr Iannis, he provides Corelli with the goat named Restitution, which is a gift to Pelagia.

Similar pairs

- **Dr Iannis and Corelli:** both are loved by Pelagia for being gifted, humane and humorous.
- **Pelagia and Dr Iannis:** a parallel to the dead father and weeping daughter in ch. 28.
- **Carlo and Velisarios:** both are gentle giants.
- **Carlo and Dr Iannis:** lay down their lives for their loved ones.
- **Pelagia and Lemoni:** young females, animal-lovers and intelligent questioners.
- **Francesco and Corelli:** beloved of Carlo for their 'impetuosities, ludicrous jests, and complete irreverence' (p. 41).
- **Arsenios and Dr Iannis:** changed by their war experience and become martyrs.
- **Carlo and Corelli:** faithful lovers and loyal comrades.
- **Pelagia and Corelli:** each wants to take the other's nationality and both are artistic.
- **Pelagia and Dr Iannis:** she 'almost became the doctor' (p. 485) and they share the writing of the 'History'.
- **Mandras and Weber:** victims of ideology, ignorance and the need to prove themselves.

- **Corelli and young Iannis:** romantics and mandolin players.
- **Francesco and Mandras:** destroyed physically and mentally by the ice war.

Contrasting pairs

- **Kokolios and Stamatis:** political opponents — communist and royalist.
- **Corelli and Mandras:** individualist and traditionalist; musician and fisherman; one loves Pelagia and the other loves the idea of her.
- **Francesco and Corelli:** 'could not be more different' (p. 119).
- **Carlo and Weber:** the hero and the coward.
- **Corelli and Weber:** have different temperaments and attitudes to humanity — Corelli's views are personal and independent, Weber's political and conformist; cat and dog respectively.
- **Dr Iannis and Mandras:** one is a writer and a liberal, the other illiterate and a dogmatist.
- **Dr Iannis and Weber:** one is a wise altruist, the other a naïve self-server.

Mythological characters

Actaeon	a human hunter torn to pieces by his own dogs after having been turned into a stag by Artemis, whom he had seen unrobed while bathing	*Demeter*	goddess of grain
		Dionysus	god of wine, intoxication and ecstasy
		Odysseus	hero of *The Iliad* and *The Odyssey*; king of Ithaca
Aegisthus	murdered Agamemnon, with the help of the latter's wife, Clytemnestra; killed in turn by Agamemnon's son Orestes	*Orion*	a hunter; blinded, he was healed by the sun, and is now among the stars
		Penelope	wife of Odysseus who patiently waited and sewed for 20 years
Aesculapius	god of healing		
Agamemnon	king of Mycenae at the time of the Trojan War; returned from the war with his mistress Cassandra	*Persephone*	daughter of Demeter; raped by Pluto, king of Hades (the Underworld)
		Philoctetes	sailor in *The Odyssey*
Aphrodite	goddess of love	*Poseidon*	god of the sea
Apollo	god of prophecy, light, poetry and music	*Sisyphus*	his fate in Hades was to roll a rock up a hill each day, only for it to roll back down
Artemis	goddess of chastity, fighting, wild animals and hunting	*Tiresias*	a blind prophet
Athene	goddess of wisdom	*Zeus*	the king of the gods of Mount Olympus
Atlas	a Titan who held up the sky		

Historical characters

Aeschylus	ancient Greek tragic playwright
Filippo Anfuso	assistant to Count Ciano (qv)
Capt. Appollonio	battery commander in the 33rd Artillery Regiment, 'Acqui' Division
Attila	the celebrated Hun warlord who terrorised Europe in the fifth century
Marshal Badoglio	chief of the Italian General Staff; dismissed for criticising the ill-advised invasion of Greece
Col. Barge	commander of the German forces on Cephallonia
Tom Barnes	New Zealand officer, member of the SOE mission to Greece
Caligula	Roman emperor, notorious for violence and self-indulgence
Constantine Cavafy	one of the greatest Greek poets of the early twentieth century
Gen. Ugo Cavallero	chief of the Italian General Staff in 1941
Count Galeazzo Ciano	Italian Foreign Minister
Empedocles	ancient Greek philosopher
Gen. Antonio Gandin	commander of the Italian 'Acqui' Division on Cephallonia
Marshal Graziani	Italian general in North Africa
Emmanuele Grazzi	Italian Ambassador to Greece

Adolf Hitler	*Der Führer*, the leader of Nazi Germany (1933–45)
Homer	ancient Greek Poet; author of *The Iliad* and *The Odyssey*
Francesco Jacomoni	Italian Ambassador in Albania; organiser of pro-Italian Albanian guerrilla groups
Eleni Karaindrou	Greek composer of film music
Constantine Karamanlis	right-wing politician who became President of Greece in 1980
Gen. Hubert Lanz	commander of the German Forces in northern Greece
Andreas Laskaratos	Greek Poet (1811–1901) from Lixouri on Cephallonia
Vladimir Lenin	leader of the 1917 Russian Revolution; author of the minor pamphlet 'What is to be done?'
Curzio Malaparte	editor of the fascist magazine *Prospettive*
Yannis Markopoulos	Greek composer of popular music
Ioannis Metaxas	colonel; dictator of Greece from 1936
Benito Mussolini	*Il Duce*, the leader of fascist Italy (1922–43)
Brig. Eddie Myers	head of the SOE Mission to the Greek resistance movements
Kostis Palamas	Greek poet (1859–1943)
Alexandros Papagos	Chief of Staff of the Greek Army

George Papandreou	Centrist Prime Minister of Greece
Pindar	ancient Greek poet, famous for Odes
Plato	ancient Greek philosopher
Plutarch	ancient Greek biographer
Pontius Pilate	Roman Emperor who reluctantly ordered the crucifixion of Christ
Gen. Visconti Prasca	commander of Italian eleventh Army invading Greece
Joachim von Ribbentrop	foreign minister of Nazi Germany
Antonio Salazar	fascist dictator of Portugal
Christos Sartzetakis	President of Greece from 1985 to 1990
Socrates	ancient Greek philosopher; forced to commit suicide by drinking hemlock as a punishment for holding unconventional views
Gen. Ubaldo Soddu	replaced Gen. Prasca in late 1940
Solon	ancient Athenian ruler
Mikis Theodorakis	Greek composer, associated with resistance to the *junta* of 1967–74
Aris [Velouchiotis]	military commander of ELAS
Eleftherios Venizelos	Prime Minister of Greece during the First World War
Napoleon Zervas	leader of EDES
King Ahmed Zog	king of Albania until the Italian invasion

Themes

The main themes of *Captain Corelli's Mandolin*, a novel about love and war, are those to do with history and memory. These themes, which may be grouped in opposing pairs, have parallels with those of Homer's *Odyssey*. Many of the tragic and comic themes of the novel are intimated in the dedication of the novel to de Bernières' parents and in the epigraph poem by Humbert Wolfe, a little-known interwar poet de Bernières hopes to revive. They both refer to the debt of gratitude owed to previous generations for their risks and sacrifices. The poem prefigures Corelli's nobility in choosing to 'smile in the face of death' but is mainly an indictment of the waste of golden youth which war turns into loss, greyness and pain.

Love and war

'The real theme [of the novel] is how do people love? And what war does is put them under pressure...stretch the fabric.'

Sister Wendy

The novel is, on one level, a traditional romantic love story between two young, beautiful people of the opposite sex whose developing relationship is threatened and thwarted by circumstances beyond their control. However, the novel could also be described as an exploration of love in all its forms. For example:

- filial (Pelagia)
- parental (Dr Iannis, Pelagia, Drosoula)
- religious (Arsenios)
- homosexual (Carlo)
- patriotic (Mandras, Kokolios, Stamatis, Dr Iannis)
- comradely (Corelli, Carlo)

Many episodes in the novel demonstrate instances of the love of:

- words (Dr Iannis)
- profession (Dr Iannis, Corelli (as composer))
- animals (Lemoni, Pelagia, Francesco, Corelli)
- music (Corelli, Pelagia, Iannis)
- beauty (Dr Iannis, Pelagia, Corelli)
- humanity (Dr Iannis, Corelli)
- life (Corelli)

On the subject of love as a phenomenon, the novel says that commitment and sacrifice define love and make it endure; it is like the entwined roots of a tree which make it 'inconceivable that you should ever part', but it is not the same as being 'in love', which any fool can do. Loving is the best thing about humanity, and it goes a long way to redeeming it from the evils humans are capable of; horrendous acts are, however, committed in its name. It is a kind of madness or miracle, defying rationality or analysis; it is a product of opportunity, accident or fate. Love can defuse anger (see ch. 31), change perceptions, create heroes and make life worth living, even when the loved one has died.

History and myth

History is the theme which binds the novel together. The novel is itself a history, it includes a History, it is about history. All the events and beliefs are either personal and political, and characters are judged by which they value more. History connects the big men with the little men. The novel spans half a century and four generations; people and places are linked by history repeating itself. The novel begins with an attempt to write history, and it gives a large slice of the real story of Cephallonia through the use of fictional characters, so fact and fiction are intertwined as history. Memory is a romanticisation of history, e.g. Pelagia claiming she had an 'Italian fiancé who was killed in the war' (p. 502). Ancient

Greek history is a framework for modern Greek history; the story of Odysseus is itself a mixture of fact and fiction. The historical cachette beneath Dr Iannis' house is closed for 36 years and links all the characters and generations to a specific time and place.

Many difficulties stand in the way of the writing of accurate history, and the novel touches on most of them. The historians and the sources are both likely to be lacking complete objectivity, and may be subject to one or more of the following disabilities: faulty memory; ethnic bias; political or religious belief; incomplete view; desire to prove preconceptions, to take a new approach or to claim victory; propaganda and deliberate misinformation; lack of any evidence; no written records; conflicting versions, misinterpreted evidence; tendencies to fictionalise; self-aggrandisement; nationalist doctrine; or fear of reprisals.

The novel includes the following examples of methods of recording public and domestic events (you should consider the objectivity and validity of each):
- historical novels, such as this one, with fictional characters
- a personal history, i.e. a subjective history book by one who is closely involved
- official history as published works by academic researchers, not participants
- story-telling in the community, so that a character's feats are passed down the generations
- forms of art, in this case turning an experience and a feeling into music
- songs, which become associated with particular people, times and places
- photographs and postcards
- personal diaries and memoirs, not intended for publication
- letters, recording feelings and relationships at a particular time, which are kept
- beloved objects which have sentimental significance and can outlive their owners
- garments and sewing
- the human body, which changes according to age and bears the scars of its owner's experiences
- individuals' memories, triggered by one of the five senses
- anniversaries: personal, national or religious
- names passed down or chosen in memory of someone
- graves and epitaphs

Public history is political; it is concerned with conflicting belief systems, and during the twentieth century these conflicts often led to war. The novel therefore has to deal, implicitly or explicitly, with the three major modern ideologies: fascism, communism and liberalism. You must decide whether de Bernières is giving an even-handed impression of these; modern communists have bitterly criticised his depiction of the Greek communists, though it can be argued that Nazism is equally condemned, and that the novel suggests the two ideologies are indistinguishable in their inhumane behaviour.

Chapter 63 on Hector and Mandras, referred to as 'Hooligans and Opportunists', presents a clear anti-communist view. However, the novel's epigraph is anti-fascist, and Carlo and Francesco reveal the iniquities of Mussolini's regime, while Weber carries the weight of anti-German feeling in the novel (though he's actually Austrian, as were all the members of the German unit on Cephallonia). The British are mildly attacked for their expediency and cynical treatment of the Greeks, but the novel's wrath is reserved for extreme regimes and militarism of either persuasion. De Bernières hated 'village Hitlers' as a pupil, as a teacher, and in the army. (He left Sandhurst and abandoned his intended military career because of his distaste for bullying.) Alexi does a spectacular volte-face from socialism to capitalism in chapter 69 out of self-interest, which suggests that de Bernières has contempt for all named ideologies and considers them a matter of opportunism or coercion rather than genuine conviction. One must conclude that the novel's position is pro-liberal, as personified by Dr Iannis and Corelli. Pelagia defines the middle position on p. 487 ('she concluded that freedom and order were not mutually exclusive, but essential preconditions of each other').

Since it is a historical novel, it is fair to consider the author's portrayal of Greeks and Italians, as de Bernières has been accused by critics of stereotyping and racism. The British, though, are equally stereotyped and treated conde-scendingly, and most of the Mussolini material is factually accurate. Humour tends to depend on stereotyping, but the Greeks in the novel are actually presented in diverse ways and as complex personalities; Mandras is very different from Dr Iannis, for instance. War could be held accountable for common behaviour traits, and the novel is a romance, among other things, which is a genre requiring clichéd situations and responses. The Italians are depicted as a homogenous group of drinking, singing womanisers, but any nation's soldiers in uniform tend to give the impression of this kind of homogeneity. Corelli is obviously more developed as a character than a stage Italian (he is not 'a typical Italian', p. 247), and Carlo Guercio is not noticeably similar to him. The novel shows admiration for most Greeks and most Italians so it might be considered unfair to accuse the novel of racist attitudes. What is clearly implied is the affinity between the Greeks and Italians, as Mediterranean peoples with similar cultures, and how there is little apparent connection between them and the northern nations, with the exception of Bunnios, who is linked through education and commitment to Greece, and who is a victim of the civil war like so many of the Greeks.

The relationship between hearsay, myth, memory and history is an inter-esting one, and it is worth considering how these concepts are represented in the novel. These natural processes create doubt and generate contrasting accounts so that the borderline between history and story is blurred. Hearsay should be balanced by the view from the other side, but usually isn't because that would spoil the story. People need to find a way to come to terms with horrifying acts, which leads them to suppress details which are intolerable, or to adapt them to a more acceptable version of events. The disturbing deaths of Carlo and Mandras are mythologised, and these pass into community folklore. As time passes, people's memories fade or give undue prominence to details which distort the overall picture. As stories are passed down the generations, they are subtly altered, like Chinese whispers. Iannis, for example, has an exaggerated belief in the powers of Velisarios and his great-grandfather.

The Greek word *historia* means story and well as history. Is it possible for the reader to distinguish between history and story in *Captain Corelli's Mandolin*? Perhaps it does not matter, as truth is often stranger than fiction, and miracles and coincidences also occur in real life. There was a real Special Operations Executive officer called Bunny Warren, a fact apparently unknown to de Bernières. Not just one miraculous escape from death occurred in the Italian massacres on Cephallonia; 34 have been documented. *The Odyssey* was fictional, but the Trojan War was real. Both history and story tell of heroism and barbarism, and therefore of humanity. One concerns itself with the big men, the other with the little men: two sides of the same coin. History is the official story of what happens unofficially; it is how we make sense of madness.

Sometimes it takes a long time for history to emerge, such as the meaning of the German text on the back of Weber's photograph which took 35 years (p. 441), and the reappearance of the living Corelli after 50 years.

Music

De Bernières is an accomplished mandolin player and really wanted to become a composer. Music is a fundamental theme of the novel, contrasted with killing. It features in the title, which stresses that his mandolin is an essential part of Corelli — the other half of himself which shares his name. Note also that both Corelli and Weber have the names of celebrated composers: Arcangelo Corelli and Carl Maria von Weber have in common with their fictional counterparts both their country of origin and their interests (see above, pp. 21–22). Antonio Corelli also has characteristics reminiscent of his namesake: he 'plays the mandolin like an angel' (p. 344).

La Scala not only supplies some of the finest comic scenes in the novel, in the tradition of Italian comic opera (La Scala is the celebrated opera house in Milan), it also serves as the only bridge between the three nations when it meets in the Doctor's house and includes Günter Weber: music transcends all differences of nationality, and is an antidote to war. The symbolism of Weber's parting gift to Pelagia of a gramophone should not be overlooked: the gramophone makes music immortal, allowing it to defeat the ravages of history and time (music can be played from beyond the grave), and it is fitting that it should be preserved in the historical cachette. He is also restoring music to Pelagia having, as he thought, torn it away by executing Corelli and the other members of La Scala, although playing it is not the same as creating it. Music bridges the classes and the rank barriers in the Italian Army, too, as all ranks of Corelli's battery could be members, dependent upon merit (musical talent) alone.

'Pelagia's March' is another key symbol. It is the image of their love, transforming war and occupation into harmony. Pelagia is twice wooed and won through music — it is 'an emotional and intellectual odyssey' for her — which is an affirmation of life. The act of creation is the positive parallel to the destruction of war, and the mandolin is the counterpart to the gun. 'Let's sing, boys' is Corelli's response to the imminence of death. Weber, by contrast, cannot sing a note. Corelli's musical talent is the equivalent to the Doctor's power of healing and Pelagia's gift for embroidery. Music is one of the ancient Greek muses and is connected to virtually every other theme and symbol of the novel, even cats, motorbikes and waistcoats.

Madness

Madness is an important theme in the novel, because 'human nature [is] fundamentally irrational to the point of insanity' (p. 487). We all have the potential for moments or periods of madness when we stand outside our normal selves (the literal meaning of the Greek word 'ecstasy'). It could be said that love and war are both acts of lunacy per se. They are both extraordinary states which cause people to lose touch with their everyday ways of perceiving and their previous values in a fervour of heightened emotion. The desire generated takes a physical form whereby a human will either resemble a god or an animal (e.g. Mandras, who does both). Madness can be a deliberate act put on to distance oneself from or to defy an unbearable reality, or an unconscious urge to return to the securities of childhood: 'Did you know that childhood is the only time in our lives when insanity is not only permitted to us, but expected?' (p. 55)

Madness can take many forms, some examples being: drunkenness; depression; despair (suicide); hallucination; lovers' antics; jokes; recklessness; impulsiveness; grief; guilt; trauma; barbarism; megalomania; possession by spirits. The Italian military campaign was a form of madness, as was Apollonio's firing on the Germans.

Most of the characters display characteristics of madness at some point in the novel:

- Mussolini — megalomania, paranoia, phobia
- Mandras — many different types, as a lover and a fighter, and on his return

- Corelli — impulsive, high-spririted, reckless, drunken, lover, 'mad son of a bitch' (p. 314), 'harebrained schemes' (p. 531)
- Francesco — delusions, despair
- Arsenios — ranting, abstinence, prophet of doom
- Bunnios — bizarre in speech and appearance
- Pelagia — depression caused by grief and guilt, belief in ghost's postcards
- Dr Iannis — refusal to speak
- Weber — 'probably in the madhouse by now' (p. 523)
- Carlo — shooting himself in the thigh, choosing to die

Kokolios, Dr Iannis and Carlo (who exhibit 'a lack of common sense' in printing the pamphlet) and the inmates of the monastery madhouse add to the comprehensive picture of insanity.

The theme of madness makes a major contribution to the structure of the novel. Both human masks, Comedy and Tragedy, are present where there is madness. A link with *The Odyssey* is established, as Odysseus had periods of madness during his voyage home, and after his arrival in Ithaca and the shedding of the blood of a hundred suitors. It is a way of suggesting that the trials of human beings can sometimes be impossible to bear as madness is a way of buying time and avoiding exposure to the full brunt of an extreme emotion, which can lead to a nervous breakdown, as in Francesco's and Pelagia's case. The kind of madness which is a permanent feature of a childlike, high-spirited, generous, innocent personality, however, is to be cherished as an individualising life-enhancing force, a refusal to bow to convention, as in Corelli's case. Because madness in the novel is in the eye of the beholder, a matter of perception, and capable of different interpretations — and because it affects both the personal and the political — it is as difficult to agree on as history itself.

Debt and sacrifice

'You owe me a life,' Pelagia says to Corelli at the end of the novel. Carlo's sacrifice for Corelli is the ultimate (as the Bible says, 'Greater love hath no man than this: that he lay down his life for his friend'). In return, Corelli owes a debt of gratitude to Carlo which he cannot repay except by the annual pilgrimage to his grave. The sacrificial goats are a premonition of the massacre of the Italian soldiers, slaughtered like animals. Weber also owes a debt of guilt for the crime that he has perpetrated, and tries to make atonement for the remainder of his life. Dr Iannis sacrifices his own life to save Pelagia in the earthquake. '"We all owe a death to nature"' says Dr Iannis to Pelagia (p. 347). War demands the sacrifice of health, youth, beauty, innocence, normality, sanity and, finally, of life itself. The little men are the ones who make the sacrifices in war, as indicated in the epigraph and dedication.

Barbarism and heroism

Two of the key contrasting themes of the novel are barbarism and heroism. Corelli and Carlo are heroes (linked to Odysseus) and Mandras would like to be but falls into barbaric behaviour because he has an 'adamantine' soul. Overcoming huge obstacles and losses can be seen as heroic (e.g. Drosoula) and it is heroic to attempt the impossible, as with Dr Iannis' Personal History, and his efforts to save the dying. Weber wants to be a heroic member of a super-race, but he is also brutalised. The massacre and burning of thousands of Italians is an extreme act of barbarism. Fascism is by definition barbaric because it is based on ignorance and intolerance. There are links with Greek mythology, in which there are heroic feats of strength and endurance, noble conduct and rituals. The Greek civil war was notorious for barbarism on both sides — for example, putting out eyes and slitting mouths. In the novel, barbarism is linked to the capacity for cruelty to animals. Heroism is brought about by individuals, and is motivated by love of some kind; barbarism is caused by rage and losing one's humanity through following a party line. Both are forms of madness in that they go beyond the limits of expected behaviour.

Death and resurrection

War, by definition, entails death. Corelli and Mandras both return from the dead twice. Farewells and partings are a kind of death, and reunions a resurrection. The symbolic opening of Carlo's grave is a resurrection. The mandolin 'dies' but lives on in Corelli's ribs, and is resurrected by Iannis. Pelagia's youth returns with Pelagia's March at the end of the novel. Objects disinterred from the cachette are resurrected. Antonia and Iannis give new life to old names. Medicine and surgery are forms of bringing people back to life. Easter, the most important Greek festival, is about death followed by resurrection. Pelagia's finishing of the History resurrects her father; the earthquake led to the creation of a new village, and the resurrection of Velisarios as strongman. Writing can live beyond death, e.g. the manuscripts of Carlo and the Doctor. There are recurring motifs of Armageddon and the Day of Judgement. History digs up the past, and mythology ensures that memory will defeat death.

The ephemeral and the eternal

The epigraph poem concerns the ephemerality of beauty, laughter and youth, and sets the tone for the novel. 'The preciousness of the ephemeral' (p. 218) may be contrasted with 'the eternal spirit of Greece' (p. 533). Pelagia and Corelli's love (and that of her parents) endures; music lasts a few minutes and for ever. The cycle of nature, seasons, and festivals keeps repeating. The next generation carries on and gives a kind of immortality, as leaves are renewed in the spring: '"You die, and then someone comes to take your place."' (p. 512); '"she will continue my life when I am gone"' (p. 430). Those who are loved live on in the perceptions of survivors: '"When loved ones die, you have to live on their behalf"' (p. 429). Individual memory is ephemeral but collective myths are eternal and outlast stone memorials.

Division and union

War both unites and divides Pelagia and Corelli; Hitler and Mussolini change from allies to enemies. Greeks and Italians come together; Germans and Italians are driven apart. Civil war is the most traumatic form of division, a self-division, as epitomised in Mandras; Stamatis and Kokolios, divided by politics, are united in the face of a greater threat. Politics create tribal loyalties which are destructive to personal relations; Pelagia and Mandras are divided by their beliefs and change from lovers to enemies. The Greek character is fundamentally divided into 'Hellene' and 'Romoi'. Love can be a union which lasts a lifetime, and beyond.

These themes, illustrated by the novel's symbols, are worth an essay in their own right, and are interwoven into the text of the novel from many perspectives and through many voices. They all link classical times to the twentieth century. Attitudes and experiences in these areas define what we mean by humanity; they touch us all and are universal. Humans have contrary impulses and contradictory sides to their character, so everything needs to contain its opposite, just as coins have two sides. In the end, de Bernières seems to be offering a comic perspective in which the positive element of each pair wins through, thanks to the indomitable spirit of a few exceptional individuals and communities, and redeems its opposite. The price, however, is waste, loss and pain, which define tragedy.

Symbols

The novel makes extensive use of symbols, i.e. objects which carry greater significance than their literal meaning, by standing for or referring to an important idea. They recur at various points, either as specific or generic items, and are one of the vehicles for the themes.

One of the ways in which this much fragmented novel is given integrity is through the use of recurring places or objects which are part of the natural or domestic environment. As in a piece of music, they fulfil the function of a keynote and they create a pattern of 'weaving trails'. They link generations, ancient and modern Greece, and force the reader to see similarities or contrasts between characters according to their different attitudes towards the same things. They are touchstones by which the characters can be divided into those we admire and those who fail the 'humanity test'. In the final chapter all the symbols are resurrected and make a reappearance.

The mandolin is a metaphor for peace and harmony, the life-enhancing opposite of a gun ('armed only with his mandolin'). It represents music as the highest pursuit of civilisation, and one which transcends cultural and national differences because it is a universal language. It is female in aspect (Corelli names it Antonia) and visually beautiful; it serves as a reminder of romantic love, stringed instruments being a traditional tool of courtship. It makes a magical sound, and can perform miracles as in Greek mythology; it literally binds Corelli together when its strings are used as surgical wire to save his life, remaining part of him thereafter. Known in Greece as the bouzouki, it is a favourite and traditional instrument in both Italy and Greece and serves as a link between the two countries.

The motorcycle is a symbol of freedom and has been widely employed as such in the twentieth century (e.g. in films such as *The Great Escape* and *Easy Rider*). It is another finely-tuned instrument with a musical rhythm; by transporting the lovers to Casa Nostra it becomes an agent of and witness to their love. The two riders are forced to sit as if conjoined, united physically by it, and this position echoes all the romantic associations of horse-riding and chivalry. It becomes a time machine when it brings the lovers together again at the end of the novel and allows them to revisit the past. The three fates ride past on a motorcycle to end the novel. (Note also that de Bernières is a passionate motorcyclist.)

The olive tree is the universal symbol of peace in the form of the olive branch. It is also the essence of the unchanging Greek and Italian landscapes; it is claimed that trees to be found in Greece today date from the era of Homer himself, and it is certainly true that they live for several hundred years. In ancient Greece the olive was revered for its longevity; the bed of Odysseus and Penelope is made from a living olive tree. Carlo is buried among the roots of the olive tree 'in the soil of Odysseus' time', and olive wood is used for the funeral pyres of the massacred Italians, just as it was in *The Odyssey* for the Greek heroes of the Trojan War. It is also, more generally, associated with continuity between past and present, joy, the pastoral idyll, nature as a provider, and Christianity (Arsenios' cross). It is the 'entwined roots' of the olive tree to which Dr Iannis refers as a metaphor for enduring love.

Cats, which include Psipsina because she is a 'funny kind of cat', are female in temperament and are beloved of Lemoni, Antonia, Pelagia and Corelli. Independent and characterful, related to lions (and the opposite of sheep), they are loathed by the insensitive and the inadequates who try to kill them in the novel. The name Psipsina lives on after the first one is clubbed to death by the Germans just for being tame, i.e. different. They are associated with magic, beauty and mystery (de Bernières dislikes servile dogs but is a great admirer of cats); they also represent the female victims of war, including whores. Cats apparently like mandolins (p. 222).

Goats are a sacrifice for the gods and are victims of war; they are also producers of milk, nature's bounty in a pastoral world, and an enduring feature of the Greek landscape since ancient times. They are the companions of the 'mountain god' Alekos. The word 'tragedy' comes from the ancient Greek for goat, but as well as being destroyers (eaters of words) in the novel they symbolise restitution, a characteristic of comedy.

Snails are vulnerable, like humans; they weave crossing silver trails like history, and are unchanged from prehistoric times, like the Greek landscape in which they live. As food, they are a reminder of the extreme poverty caused by war. Snail-hunting is the occasion of the first real kiss between Corelli and Pelagia and becomes the symbol of their love affair and reunion.

The bedcover is a symbol of Pelagia's doomed engagement; parallel to Penelope's shroud, it is 'never bigger than a towel', and actually gets smaller as her love for the 'much-diminished' (p. 166) Mandras fades. Psipsina is sick on it and the goat eats it, suggesting a lack of sympathy between Mandras and domestic animals. Weaving is a typical domestic pursuit of rural Greek women through the ages and the bedcover reminds us of the bed as a symbol of birth, marriage and death, the three significant points of the human life cycle and therefore of personal history. The bedcover 'burgeons' when Corelli becomes the inspiration.

The waistcoat is Pelagia's love offering: Mandras rejects it because it is imperfect; Corelli accepts it as a flawed but beautiful gift, thereby proving their compatability. It depicts the Greek landscape of 'languid flowers, soaring eagles, leaping fish'; it lasts 50 years, as long as Corelli's love, and the wearing of it links the young and old Corellis. Being asymmetrical, it is a celebration of life; 'symmetry is only a property of dead things' (p. 215). Like Corelli's music, it turns nature into art.

The cachette is a time capsule which represents personal history, memory as preserved in possessions. It is also a kind of grave for Corelli and the mandolin, so that the opening of the cachette is not only a resurrection of strength for Velisarios, but also conjures the 'ghost' of Corelli and is a parallel event to the opening of Carlo's grave. It acts as a link between the generations and life before and after the earthquake which it survives. Reunion with the objects is a restitution for Pelagia.

Ice is white death; it has, like Mandras, 'adamantine inflexibility' and is nature's weapon of destruction. It contrasts with the warmth and colour of normal life on a Greek island and is the antithesis to the life-sustaining sea. It drives men mad and makes myths and monsters. It kills Mandras' soul and takes Francesco from Carlo; it is the agent of the Italian nemesis in Albania, and represents the war and cold inhumanity of political expediency.

Dolphins are mentioned in *The Odyssey*, and in this novel they have a mythical significance as sensitive sea creatures with whom Mandras, the innocent fisherman, can sport naked and appear as a Greek god. Dolphins are the only creatures he loves unreservedly, because they don't judge him and they come when he calls their names. They symbolically receive his body — rejected by even his closest human relatives — on behalf of the sea and elevate him to legendary status. Three is a mystical number in religion and literature. The sea is Mandras's element first and last: warm and forgiving, the antithesis to ice and associated with birth, baptism and cleansing.

Symbolic events

These are the recurring events in the novel:

Healing is a miracle and a resurrection which Dr Iannis performs on many occasions, though he is not a trained doctor. It is a Christian concept and an expression of altruism; it represents the life force and is a gift of the gods. It employs ancient Greek herbal remedies, thus operating in partnership with nature and the environment, and illustrating the ability of humans to survive and recover.

Feats of strength are superhuman and therefore godlike. Both Carlo and Velisarios carry their 'brothers' when in trouble; they represent the greatness of little men in contrast to weakness of 'great men'. They provide a clear link to Homeric heroes and Greek mythology (Atlas) as well as the Cephallonian giants who guarded Odysseus. They connect with the performance of miracles and displays of endurance and faith.

Explosions occur on an ascending scale: Velisarios's cannon, the jeep engine, Francesco's death, the 'spiky rustball', the attack on Argostoli and finally the earthquake. Fire is introduced with the assault on the watchtower, forms the message of Arsenios' prophesies, and culminates in the mass burning of Italian bodies on a funeral pyre (again, an echo of Homer); Corelli finally becomes a fireman (the opposite of a soldier). Prometheus stole fire from the gods and it

is a dangerous and destructive element in the novel, linked to Armageddon and hell. It is used to destroy historical evidence.

Homecoming — Mandras returns twice, Dr Iannis once, Corelli annually and then for good; homecoming is the culmination of *The Odyssey*. Time spent in exile and experiences elsewhere change humans drastically and reinforce the emotional significance of home — Casa Nostra. Carlo finds a final resting place in the ancient Greek soil; Mandras goes home to the sea; Pelagia adopts Italy.

Style and register

Captain Corelli's Mandolin shares some characteristics of a postmodern text in that it does not have one narrative viewpoint, but incorporates many, according to the background and perspective of the observer or speaker.

Because the novel also contains examples of many different styles and registers, one of the central questions for anyone studying the text is that of identifying the author's voice. Prior to postmodernism, the author's voice and her or his ideas and attitudes were usually apparent and even intrusive, whereas in a contemporary text the authorial voice may be camouflaged, but still detectable, as in chapter 1 in which the events are related from the perspective of Dr Iannis, but the narrator comments on his character. This chapter is characterised linguistically by extensive use of medical terminology, which creates humour because of its incongruity, and reveals the difference in education between the Doctor and the rest of the village. It establishes the Doctor as a wise and gifted healer and introduces the theme of miraculous recoveries — suggesting from the outset that the Doctor will represent the liberal, ironic and humane viewpoint of the author and of the novel.

The authorial voice of the novel has been described as being full of 'elegant Latinate constructions'. This presumably means long, complex sentence structures with unusual word order, and elevated diction with Latin roots. Look for evidence of this in the rare chapters which are unequivocally authorial (e.g. ch. 62 and the first part of ch. 63). More commonly, the narrative voice adopts the views and registers of the characters; the Doctor and Carlo come closest to authorial register (the Doctor speaks and writes elegantly and eruditely; Carlo uses educated, polysyllabic diction, e.g. ch. 6). It is an added linguistic complexity to the novel that all the dialogue and thought processes are meant to be in Greek or Italian, not English.

The forms of language employed in the novel range from crude sexual oaths to the lyricism of classical poetry. Here is a list of some of the registers and styles which appear: blasphemy; parody; stream of consciousness; rhetoric; satire; sarcasm; irony; elegy; eulogy; sermon; Middle English; epic; love lyric; history book; teasing; hectoring; propaganda; bombast; flirtation; flippancy; melodrama; nostalgia.

One contentious aspect of the novel is its use of words and phrases from Greek and Italian, and to a lesser extent from other languages, often without a translation. It could be argued that this gives a flavour of authenticity to the writing, or that it is merely pretentious, or that perhaps it is a mixture of both. (Bear in mind that at least some of the phrases will not be understood by the average reader, and not all of the expressions are correct!) De Bernières' purpose might be to increase the realism of his characterisation, and a more convincing creation of the Greek environment than would otherwise be possible. The use of different languages also illustrates the clash of cultures (where misunderstandings occur), and often includes examples of crude and puerile male language, presumably thought to be fitting for soldiers and villagers.

Another manifestation of the postmodernist disregard for convention and expectation is the comical treatment of serious or sentimental events: examples of which are madness, theft, the mine explosion, Mussolini's cat-killing, and the reunion of Pelagia and Corelli. Anything can be made comic, even death, by distancing the reader from the pain and the desire to empathise, and by exaggerating its farcical appearance. Comedy and tragedy are not fixed: they are just different points of view on the same event, and the absurd is always lurking. The novel seems to be pandering to conventional responses in some cases, and subverting them in others, and the reader is teased and caught out on many occasions, e.g. in ch. 26, when we are amused by the sabotage of Carlo's jeep until we learn that it claimed the life of a young tenor in La Scala who was longing to return to his sweetheart in Italy.

The diversity of registers and styles employed in the novel represent the full range of possible human emotions and responses. Inconsistency is the key feature of the novel, and is manifested in every possible aspect of it; it is the only consistent thing about it. This suggests that history, memory, feelings and so on cannot be woven into a homogenous piece of cloth, or matching waistcoat. There are as many ways of seeing and expressing as there are viewpoints or viewers; history is an amalgam of the experiences of all relevant participants. Different styles and registers reflect different emotional states. Character is partly a matter of choice of language; therefore there will be as many styles as there are people, and types of people can differ in the extreme, e.g. Bunny Warren and Mussolini. Values are embodied in language, and therefore register and style are moral choices as well as personality indicators — this is illustrated particularly well by Arsenios. The effects of indoctrination can be made apparent by the adoption of a hegemonic style, e.g. Hector talks like a Leninist textbook.

In postmodernist literary terms, the traditional concepts of omniscient author and authorial voice are subverted by diversity.

Genre and structure

The plot of *Captain Corelli's Mandolin* interweaves two strands: the personal stories of a small number of members of an unnamed Cephallonian village, centring on Dr Iannis and his daughter Pelagia; and the public, historical story of the Greek involvement in the Second World War and the Italian occupation of the Ionian Islands following the Greek defeat by the Germans. It is the interplay between the two worlds which gives the novel its peculiar power and moving qualities: the story of lovers tragically separated by circumstances is a familiar one but, as in this case, the setting and the skill of the novelist can make it seem fresh. The Second World War has become a fertile source for novelists in recent years, with personal pathos enhanced by the backdrop of the horror of war. The little-known holocaust of the German slaughter of the Italians in 1943 gives an additional poignancy to the historical situation. The Cephallonia the tourists see, including the Italian, German and British ones, is ironically different from the underlying historical reality and the local perspective of the suffering yet enduring Greek islanders.

Of the 73 chapters of the book, the first 63 take place during the relatively short period from summer 1940 to autumn 1944. The following 10 chapters may be seen as a kind of coda, necessary for the author to complete the plot-lines and pattern he has woven, but passed over so swiftly and with so little narrative detail that they can hardly be compared with the earlier part, and many readers have found them disappointing.

The novel consists of a wide variety of styles, registers, genres and viewpoints. It is difficult to think of a kind of writing or recording which is not represented, and all categories of text appear: dialogue, monologue, narrative, descriptive, informative, reflective, lyrical, discursive and argumentative. Each chapter has a title, something which is increasingly uncommon in novels. The titles themselves represent a range of genres and literary periods (e.g. ch. 18 and ch. 37, which are deliberately archaic in style). It is instructive to look at the list of chapter titles and identify the genres of as many as you can. You will find that they include: dramatic monologue; internal monologue; letters; testament; sub-text; parody; historical overview. Embedded within the chapters is an even wider range of sub-genres, e.g. documentary, children's language, music critical review, postcard message, songs and poems, telephone conversations, proverbs and folklore, memoranda, quotations from books or potential books, propaganda, funeral oration and sermon. They also demonstrate the interweaving of separate narratives, especially those in several parts ('L'Omosessuale', 'The Good Nazi', 'Liberating the Masses'). Some titles are obvious while others are more obscure; they shift between the personal and the political. Both fictional and historical characters appear in the chapter titles and the ironic structural juxtaposition of the big men and the little men makes a thematic point.

Captain Corelli's Mandolin has interwoven narrative lines of a love story and a war story, so that the full range of reader response can be evoked and there is something for everyone. Love becomes more vulnerable and precious against a background of hostilities, and war becomes more threatening and poignant when a relationship is at stake. War is political, love is personal, but these universal and perpetual human experiences can become confused or intertwined, and are two sides of the same coin, e.g. 'Pelagia's March' unites the martial and the lyrical. For each of the characters, their views on passion and conflict define their personality and philosophy of life. Though seemingly opposites, love and war are in some ways strangely similar, and can be used in ironic juxtaposition as manifestations of 'delirium'. Both involve two parties and require commitment, sacrifice and a willingness to give oneself up to extremes of emotional and physical sensation. They can both lead to disappointment, death, enmity, revenge, moments of joy and triumph, and moments of pathos and heartbreak. Both are beyond the normal rules of justice: all's fair in love and war.

Postmodernism

One reason for the multiplicity of genres in *Captain Corelli's Mandolin* is that it shares some stylistic features of the literary movement known as postmodernism (see also Style and Register, p. 63). The postmodernist writer rejects traditional and large-scale historical interpretations, such as Marxism, which have enslaved large parts of the world by being absolute and universal, suggesting that small-scale, modest, local narratives are needed to replace them and to restore humanity, and preferring provisional, little stories which are strong enough to guide us but which make no claims beyond the here and now. This would seem to be the message of *Captain Corelli's Mandolin*, in which the wholesome personal philosophies of Captain Corelli and Dr Iannis are opposed to the destructive political ideologies of Marx/Lenin/Hector or Nietzsche/Hitler/Weber. De Bernières has himself made a number of comments in connection with the novel which seem to support this view: 'History ought to consist of the anecdotes of the little people who are caught up in it'; 'Looking back on the things that I've published, it seems I'm rather obsessed with the question of power, I seem to be very interested in the abuse of it.'

In some ways it seems that de Bernières has fallen back on the trusted plot formula of a love affair fraught with opposition and against a background of war which would have appealed to nineteenth-century readers and opera lovers. The novel covers fifty years in the same location, which is a means in traditional novels of following the lives of several generations of the same family. What is clearly influenced by late twentieth-century writing, however, is the form and structure of the novel: there is no strictly chronological plot, consistent viewpoint, or uniformity of style. Story and history can be conveyed in other modes than the standard technique of omniscient narrator in the past tense with interludes of character dialogue. A postmodernist text is a multi-dimensional collage which reveals that there are many ways of seeing, depending on who you are, where you are looking from, and your social and historical conditioning.

Another way in which the novel resists traditional rules is the creation of 'faction', a mixture of fiction and fact, as demonstrated by the use of both real historical and fictitious characters. The novel happily juxtaposes Mussolini with Corelli and Metaxas with Mandras, as if they were equal participants in the historical process. Some minor characters' names are real, such as Myers and Gandin, and some are not, like all the Cephallonians. Although many people have claimed to be or to have known the 'real' Captain Corelli, de Bernières is adamant that he had no such person in mind. But is de Bernières writing a history or a story? This is a question which all readers of the text need to ask.

One aspect of the book's structure which is very clear, and which has led to criticism, is de Bernières' determination to make the plot cover four generations. This requires the reunion of Corelli and Pelagia to take place in 1993, fifty years after the massacre, and to achieve this the author has to rely upon some rather dubious devices. Corelli supposedly returned to Cephallonia every year, but never asked anybody whether Pelagia was really married or whose the baby was. He lived in Athens as a Greek citizen for 25 years but did not bother to make himself known to Pelagia until they were both in their seventies. However, the supposed benefits of the elapsing of such a long expanse of time are meant to outweigh the reader's frustration (and possible incredulity), and it is a perfectly feasible and admirable character trait of Corelli that he would not wish to upset Pelagia's life if she had married someone else.

Romanticism

The two fundamental features of literature in classical, Biblical and medieval times (and onwards) have always been love and war. The word 'chivalrous', which defines the perfect courtly lover of the Middle Ages, comes from the French for 'soldier on horseback', and the tales of King Arthur and his knights are concerned in equal measure with battles and seductions. Many literary heroines through the ages have played Penelope's role of the wife/lover who waits and pines for a hero away at a war in a distant land. At the same time, there have been many soldier/lover characters in fiction willing to live bravely and die gloriously for their mistress and/or their country. In medieval literature, winning a lady's heart was seen in terms of besieging a city, breaching the wall and conquering the citadel, and rival male claimants for a woman had to prove themselves worthy by jousting in tournaments to impress her with their military skills and thus win her approval as a suitor. The novel belongs chiefly to this genre of romance.

The literary period called Romanticism began in the late eighteenth century. It is most commonly associated with the Romantic poets such as Wordsworth, Coleridge and Keats and was in some respects a resurrection of medievalism. In a reversal of previous doctrine, feelings rather than reason are to be trusted, impulses followed are safer than rules obeyed. The Romantics championed the cause of the rebellious individual and of the little man who stood up to giants. The settings for Romantic writing are almost exclusively outdoors and in unspoilt countryside. Nature is a life force to be respected and revered; those who cut themselves off from her, and mistreat animals, for instance, will perish spiritually. Love can be expressed with a flower and memory can be attached to a tree, since nature symbolises aspects of the human heart.

Mysticism is one of the elements of the Romantic philosophy, which propounds the view that not everything can or should be explained by logic or science; some apparently surprising events, such as coincidences and miracles — which are part of general human experience for the observant, receptive person — should just be seen as the symbolic workings of the natural order, whatever one wishes to call it. This is different from magic, which implies a supernatural and fantastical event which cannot be assimilated to life as we know it. De Bernières has denied that there is any magic in *Captain Corelli's Mandolin* (although he used it in previous novels), but some critics have claimed that unnatural coincidences and patterns are evident in the novel, and cite the opening of Carlo's grave as a prime example.

In Romantic literature there is an overwhelming sense of ephemerality, of the transience and ravages of time, which steals youth and destroys innocence and betrays hopes. For this reason there is a preoccupation with the ideal of an early but beautiful death in order to avoid the horrors of pain, old age and physical and emotional decay. Mandras dies romantically, returning to Nature, innocence and a state of former beauty. Beauty and passion and free will are the gods of Romanticism, and enslavement to a system the ultimate evil. The arts therefore play an important role in the Romantic world view, since music and poetry are acts of creation and statements of independence capable of evoking the deepest emotion and providing inspiration to others.

Fairy tales were favoured as plot sources by Romantic writers who appreciated the mystery created by such events as finding an abandoned baby on a doorstep or an anonymous letter. Pelagia wishes for a time-machine, Iannis needs a giant to open a trap door, and both miraculously appear. There are many such events in *Captain Corelli's Mandolin*, which is based on a series of sudden disappearances and unannounced or disguised returns, promises made and anniversaries observed. There are feats of great strength and moments of torture; things lost and things found. These elements are in ironic counterpoint to the harsh realities of domestic life or the hollow gestures of political leaders, as well as serving to trick the reader into expecting a fairytale ending for Pelagia and Corelli.

In addition the 'eternal triangle' concept of 'three into two won't go' is applicable to the war situation as well as to the rival lovers, since Germany and Italy both want Greece and are prepared to fight over her. This provides material for inevitable tragedy, since someone has to lose and much conflict and heartache will be produced along the way. *Romeo and Juliet* is based on this plot formula, as are many other Shakespeare plays, and it is still a common storyline in soap opera, the modern descendant of the romance tradition. Mandras and Antonio Corelli are suitors and soldiers competing for the hand and love of the attractive maiden Pelagia. Traditionally the reader takes the side of the forbidden rival who is beloved rather than the one with a prior or more orthodox entitlement.

Comedy, tragedy and humour

The novel conspicuously juxtaposes the comic and the tragic, includes a great deal of humour, and often surprises the reader by treating humorously episodes which are inherently serious. A wide range of types of humour are to be found, many of them vulgar and crude. Only the Doctor and Corelli are witty or intentionally ironic. De Bernières seems to wish to shock the reader by his lavatorial and obscene language, but he would probably claim simple realism and the desire to cover the full scope of human experience and response.

Sometimes the humour derives from situational ironies, for example: Carlo and Francesco are awarded secret medals for killing their fellow soldiers (and were themselves supposed to be killed); Arsenios doesn't enjoy his gifts of wine in his confined circumstances; Pelagia tries to hate Corelli but instead falls in love with him; the engineer has his head blown off, though he alone urged proper precautions for the mine detonation; Pelagia beats Corelli with a broom at their reunion; Stamatis wants the pea put back in his ear; Corelli buys a goat for milking which turns out to be male.

The reader is probably most surprised by the instances of black humour — when a serious subject, like death or war, is made fun of: 'I have related these things as though they were amusing…' (p. 119). Black or sick humour is subversive as it breaks taboos and draws attention to the paradoxical nature of human responses to events. It provides the necessary distance to make the unbearable more bearable, and stresses the absurdity of war. Examples are Mussolini's cat-killing; Mandras being injured twice; the explosion of the 'spiky rustball'; civil war atrocities as reported by Myers; Mussolini's criminal record.

Another characteristic form of humour is satire, a form of mockery through exaggeration or parody, which ridicules or shows contempt for someone or something. Examples are the Italian army, which is disorganised, ineffectual and ineptly led; the Greek church, portrayed as hypocritical and self-indulgent; Mussolini, who is a 'ludicrous buffoon', a 'moral and intellectual pygmy', vain and immature; the British, seen as self-righteous and complacent, with ridiculous speech and an obsession with tea.

The alternation and juxtaposition of comic and tragic episodes is both a structural and thematic device. Some chapters are a mixture of both, for example:

- ch. 8: the pine marten is saved eventually, though her death seems inevitable
- ch. 23: Mandras' madness is treated humorously but then it becomes more threatening
- ch. 43: the explosion is farcical and Corelli survives, but a wiser onlooker is killed
- ch. 44: moves from farce to lament as the goat is discovered missing and presumed dead

In the novel as a whole there are a similar number of comic and tragic events, but there are more comic scenes at the beginning and end, whereas the middle part is fairly unremitting destruction and sorrow. This is the effect of war and occupation, which bring family division, physical and mental trauma, and permanent loss. Ordinary people have to pay for the gestures and mistakes of the public figures.

The novel shows suffering, ageing, hunger, loss, waste, guilt, treachery, betrayal, fear and self-interest, while apathetic gods look on. However, 'we humans are blameless' (p. 173) and the human spirit, exemplified by music, survives and triumphs. Dolphins exist, Corelli redeems Mandras, Dr Iannis redeems Weber, the priest redeems himself, and (like the priest and Mandras) men are seen as gods as well as beasts. Promises are kept, love is fulfilled unto death, sacrifices are made, faith achieves miracles, obstacles are overcome, the pie is still made without the meat, sheep can become lions, 'Cephallonia doesn't sink, it floats' (p. 475), villages are rebuilt, personal histories get finished, babies arrive miraculously to childless women, Pelagia finds love, and *The Odyssey* has a happy ending. War saves individuals and brings people together as well as destroying communities and separating families ('it was the war that brought us together and the war that prises us apart,' p. 307), makes saints as well as victims, brings out the best as well as the worst ('Drosoula's spirit was unbroken,' p. 445).

There is 'the invincible power of…humanitarian impulse' (p. 456), 'Some things change for the better' (p. 521), we can sing and 'smile in the face of death' (p. 396), 'the eternal spirit of Greece' lives on (p. 533). As Homer puts it, 'Men in their generations are like the leaves of the trees. The wind blows and one year's leaves are scattered to the ground; but the trees burst into bud and put on fresh ones when the springtime comes.' (*The Iliad Book VI*; ll. 415–16)

Technically, the novel has a comic resolution, with reunion, eating, joking, music, and recovery of what was lost (restitution). However, readers may want to argue that fifty years is too much of a lifetime's debt to be repaid, that youth and beauty were lost and cannot be replaced, and that the relationship will never be consummated or produce children. Alternative plot developments could have been Corelli dying at any point or choosing not to return, Pelagia's death, or the misunderstanding over Pelagia's baby never being cleared up. For some readers, any of these would be preferable — either more romantic or more realistic.

Previews and prophecies

An important and repeated structural device in the novel is the use of previews or prophecies of events which later take place. Here are some examples:
- Psipsina is nearly clubbed by a German, and later is thus killed
- Dr Iannis predicts that Pelagia will marry a foreigner
- premonitions of the earthquake in the explosions
- references to apocalypse and fire prepare for the incineration of the Italians

Some effects of using this device include dramatic irony, in that the reader knows more than characters do, and the creation of tension. Prophecy is widely used in classical literature and is a link with Homer; it gives the impression that fate is in control and that people are the victims of circumstance, creating pathos and empathy with the characters. It reflects historical hindsight and gives coherence to a fragmented novel by adding to the pattern of recurrences.

In addition, some characters are embodiments of the concept of foresight: 'Every Parting is a Foretaste of Death' (ch. 61); Arsenios becomes a prophet warning of the Day of Judgement; Drosoula is a forerunner of the old Pelagia; Pelagia is an intimation of the old Lemoni; the young Corelli prefigures himself fifty years later; Carlo predicts his own death; Pelagia foresees Mandras drowning. The household of three women previews the final vision in the novel of the three women on the back of a motorcycle, and are in turn previewed by Mandras conflating Cephallonia, the Virgin Mary and Pelagia.

The idea of foresight and hindsight ties in closely with some of the novel's themes. Foresight is miraculous if the outcome is correctly predicted; it is a god-like ability which suggests the inevitability of fate. Everything can be predicted because history repeats itself; the future becomes the past, e.g. Carlo's last letter to Corelli. The past (and myth) influences expectations of the present. Life consists of attempts to predict the future, e.g. when choosing a marriage partner; parents plan and worry about their children's futures. A promise is a commitment to the future; the aim of fiction is to keep the reader engaged in a game of prediction. *The Odyssey* contains many examples of curses, vows and prophecies, and the novel ends with a vision of the future of the 'eternal spirit of Greece' and of a concerto.

Hindsight and repetition

History is founded on hindsight and the novel begins with Dr Iannis revisiting the trials of Cephallonia through the ages; hindsight changes our perception which is therefore not fixed. An example is the revaluation of a character many years later because of new information, such as Carlo's homosexuality and the revaluation of the Italians as friends, not enemies, when compared to the German occupiers. Even the war became 'piffling' compared to the earthquake. Only with hindsight can we know when we were happy and what we have lost; therefore it is the cause of elegy, tragedy, nostalgia. Odysseus constantly thinks of his past and his home; story-telling is a matter of hindsight, narrated in the past tense — like a novel.

There are also a significant number of repetitions or parallels in the novel: here are some examples.

- Dr Iannis 'stole' his wife who was engaged to another
- Carlo's love for Francesco is transferred to Corelli
- two countries occupy Cephallonia in succession
- Mandras goes to fight twice
- Mandras twice orders Pelagia to read her letters to him
- Antonia, Psipsina and Iannis are all names used twice
- Spiridon is the second mandolinist
- there are two goats and two 'cats' as pets
- the manuscript of the History is eaten twice
- Mandras goes naked into the sea twice
- Carlo has two funerals
- Corelli is twice inspired to compose
- 'History repeats itself, first as tragedy, and then again as tragedy.' (p. 441)

The use of repetition suggests that history is cyclical and inevitable, and makes patterns like threads in a woven cloth. Recurrences force the reader to confront the passing of time and to make connections and comparisons.

Finally, what does the patchwork of genres convey as a message about history, life and literature? What is lost by having no omnipresent authorial voice or consistent viewpoint? Suggestions might be that 'faction' is an inextricable mixture of fact and fiction, and history is an amalgam of myth, memory and statistics.

These elements are themselves a blend of reality and wishful thinking, as the novel shows. Recycling of events as stories is a feature of literature and life, and oral and written records are equally subjective. Contrasting and contradictory views give the full picture and expose the fallacy of an 'omniscient' narrator or a supposedly objective historian. Interpretations of history, life and literature all depend on who, when, where and why; social, political, geographical and cultural conditioning are factors which determine outcomes and evaluations, however hard we try to prove otherwise: 'History Itself Was Impossible.' (p. 341)

The Odyssey parallel

The two great epic poems of Homer, *The Iliad* and *The Odyssey*, dating from the seventh century BC but relating events which took place 500 years earlier, form the foundation of all subsequent western literature. *The Iliad* is concerned with the 10-year Trojan War (caused by the rape and abduction of the Greek queen Helen by the Trojan prince Paris), and the defeat and destruction of the city of Troy by the Greeks, who employed the celebrated Trojan Horse to enter the city. *The Odyssey* tells the story of the wanderings of the Greek hero Odysseus on his 10-year voyage home to the island of Ithaca or, possibly, Cephallonia. *Captain Corelli's Mandolin* has many explicit parallels with *The Odyssey* — and others which are implicit and which may not be recognised by a reader unfamiliar with Homer's work — which permeate the whole novel and provide the links between twentieth-century Cephallonia and ancient Greece.

The return voyage of Odysseus from Troy to his home is an archetype of the heroic quest; he has to overcome numerous obstacles and temptations but remains ultimately true to his purpose and essentially loyal to his faithful wife, Penelope, waiting at home for him and fending off importunate suitors. Mandras at first plays the role of Odysseus but later, when he is discredited, it is Corelli who takes on the role of the patient hero, lover and warrior.

There are eleven references to Homer or the Trojan War in the novel, and the name of Odysseus is used seven times. Specific parallels of which the reader should be aware are:

- **Mandras** volunteers to go and fight for the honour of his country, leaving behind his beloved. During his long and circuitous return from the war, he is waylaid in a cave by a one-eyed witch named Circe (ch. 22), a conflation of the witch of that name and the Cyclops in *The Odyssey*; this is the most explicit comparison in the novel. When he finally returns to Pelagia's house, she (like Penelope) does not recognise him, but the faithful pet does (in Odysseus' case, his dog; Psipsina in ch. 20).

- **Corelli**'s parallels with Odysseus include his character: he is honourable, mad, sensitive, flamboyant, loyal and courageous. He returns 'home' to Penelope/Pelagia long after it could reasonably be expected; he is loved by men and women, children, animals and gods. He is a wily trickster, a dreamer and a storyteller/artist. Drawn into a war he has no heart for and has to fight in a foreign land, he nonetheless shows loyalty to his comrades and the cause. He suffers homesickness for Greece, the nostalgia much stressed in *The Odyssey*.
- **Pelagia**, in Mandras' absence, sews an article which never grows, just as Penelope each day wove a shroud which she unravelled each evening. She hears no word of her lover/husband's survival or return, and finds it difficult to believe when he reappears. She is also a Helen of Troy figure in that she is stolen by a foreigner from her Greek husband-to-be.
- **Carlo**, a giant, is a reminder of the fictional giants of Cephallonia in Homer's time; his body is buried in 'the soil of Odysseus' time' (ch. 58). His dedication to his beloved comrades in arms, first Francesco and then Corelli, is reminiscent of the noble behaviour of the Greek heroes of the Trojan War.
- **Father Arsenios** is like the doomed prophet Cassandra, who is fated to foretell the catastrophic future, including the fall of Troy, but is not believed.
- **Drosoula** plays a similar role to the aged Anticlea, the down-to-earth, devoted and motherly servant of Penelope who supports her in her long wait.

Author's comments

Louis de Bernières has participated in a television documentary and written newspaper articles. Below is a collection of his comments on the novel and his critics which offer insight and a starting point for discussion. They could also be referred to in essays, though remember that it is the reader's response which matters, not the author's views.

- 'My Dr Iannis stands for something — he is a brave man — he has a lot of love in his heart... Almost everybody in that [novel] is motivated by love.'
- 'History ought to consist of the anecdotes of the little people who are caught up in it.'
- 'History is personal, war is personal.'
- 'I am generally optimistic about life. I generally like human beings wherever I go.'
- 'I like to tackle classical themes in literature.'
- 'I'm pretty much old-fashioned in this respect... You do have heroes, you have people who are decent and brave and have fine feelings. They are not to be thought of as naïve.'

- 'After I'd finished the book, I was in fact a little bit worried about whether Corelli was a properly rounded character, because he was more of an invention than, for example, Dr Iannis.'
- 'I wish I'd been a composer instead of a writer.'
- 'I like to choose names that suit people...Pelagia — ocean current — goes in a circle and comes back to the start.'
- 'Love is the hardest thing to write about.'
- 'You can't really write an honest book in which people are unmotivated by love.'
- 'Looking back on the things that I've published, it seems I'm rather obsessed with the question of power, I seem to be very interested in the abuse of it. *Captain Corelli's Mandolin* was really about what happens to ordinary people when megalomaniacs get busy. The ordinary lives of ordinary people get destroyed when powerful people get big ideas.'
- 'The book became too successful for its own good.'
- 'There is always room for legitimate historical debate.'
- 'Some journalists absolutely cannot conceive of authors being able to invent from their own imagination.'
- [There has been a] 'torrent of brainless and trivial embuggerance which has, more than once, made me regret ever having written the book.'
- 'I don't think anyone has anything worth saying until they are in their thirties.'
- 'Violence is only used for moral effect' [in my novels.]
- [Communism is] 'the biggest failure and disappointment since the non-return of Christ.'

Quotations

Look up the following useful quotations to find out who is talking and about whom or what. Select the most useful, i.e. the multi-purpose ones, and either learn them or make sure you could find them quickly in the exam. You may wish to add others of your own; keep them brief and consider how they could be used in exam essays or coursework.

p. 8   '...all Cephallonians are poets.'

p. 20   ...everyone admires strength and is seduced by it.

p. 29   Love would inspire him.

p. 34   '...perhaps I have been nothing but an absurd little man.'

p. 34   'Everything ends in death.'

p. 34   It is honour that breathes life into the corpse when evil times have passed.

p. 215	'Symmetry is only a property of dead things.'
p. 218	...the preciousness of the ephemeral.
p. 224	...there was something about music that had never been revealed to her before: it was not merely the production of sweet sound; it was, to those who understood it, an emotional and intellectual odyssey.
p. 235	Captain Antonio Corelli woke up feeling guilty as usual.
p. 251	The unfortunate truth was that, Italian invader or not, he made life more various, rich and strange.
p. 261	'Invaders should behave with more dignity.'
p. 305	'I am not a natural parasite.'
p. 330	Prodding at the snails, she was saddened by the cruelty of a world in which the living can only live by predation on creatures weaker than themselves; it seemed a poor way to order a universe.
p. 314	...mad son of a bitch.
p. 326	'I swear on the life of my mother, I will find you another goat.'
p. 343	'Love is a kind of dementia.'
p. 345	'Love itself is what is left over when being in love has burned away.'
p. 346	'When we are mad we lose control of ourselves. We become driven.'
p. 348	'He is a good man. He knows that he is in a bad position.'
p. 350	'I don't have the advantage of thinking that other races are inferior to mine.'
p. 351	'That is my morality. I make myself imagine that it's personal.'
p. 352	'The man's mad...but he's got nightingales in his fingers.'
p. 352	It was something fine and glorious amid the loss and separation, the deprivation and fear.
p. 370	He wanted to reach out from beyond the grave and comfort her, even though he was not yet dead.
p. 382	'If you are court-martialled, I shall demand the honour of being tried alongside you.'
p. 384	...if you had died I would have gone mad, and I now thank God that I shall die before you, so that I shall not have to bear the grief.
p. 390	With a sense of tragedy in his heart such as he had never known before, he carefully arranged the child's hair.
p. 391	The unspeakable enormity of this war broke his heart...He touched his lips to his fingers, and then his fingers to the dead lips of the foreign child.
p. 392	'There has been no honour in this war, but I have to be with my boys.'
p. 396	Why not smile in the face of death?
p. 397	'I forgive you. If I do not, who will?'
p. 406	Leutnant Weber...was not the only Nazi maddened and broken by his own dutiful atrocities.

Literary terms

Assessment Objective 1 requires 'insight appropriate to literary study, using appropriate terminology'. The terms below are relevant when writing about *Captain Corelli's Mandolin* and will aid concise argument and precise expression.

antithesis	contrast of ideas expressed by parallelism
bathos	sudden change of register or content from the sublime to the ridiculous, usually to create a comic effect
caricature	grotesquely exaggerated portrayal of a person
contextuality	historical, social and cultural background of a text

cliché	predictable and overused expression or situation
closure	a sense of an ending, tying up the ends in a fictional work
elegy	lament for the death or permanent loss of someone or something
ephemeral	transitory, short-lived
epic	long narrative poem telling a tale of heroic achievements
epigraph	inscription at the head of a chapter or book
epiphany	sudden revelation of a significant truth; divine manifestation
epistolary	taking the form of letters
farce	impromptu buffoonery to excite laughter
genre	type of form or writing
intertextuality	relationship between one text and another
irony	language intended to mean the opposite of the words actually expressed; or an amusing or cruel reversal of a situation which is expected, intended or deserved
juxtaposition	placing side by side for (ironic) contrast of interpretation
legend	story about a historical figure which exaggerates their qualities or feats
lyrical	expression of strong feelings, usually love; suggestive of music
monologue	extended speech or thought process by one character
mysticism	having spiritual significance
myth	fiction about supernatural beings
paradox	self-contradictory truth
parody	ridicule by imitation and exaggeration of a style of speaking or writing
pastiche	literary composition made up of fragments of different styles
pastoral	innocent and idyllic rural existence, associated with Arcadia in ancient Greece
pathos	sad situation which evokes pity from the reader
plurality	possible multiple meanings of a text
postmodern	contemporary literary period, beginning around 1950
register	type of expression, level of formality
romance	popular story of love and war, deriving from medieval court life and fairy tale
Romanticism	influential literary movement, of the late eighteenth and early nineteenth centuries, in favour of rebellious assertion of the individual; a sense of the sublime and infinite; belief in spiritual correspondence between man and nature
satire	exposes to ridicule the vice or foolishness of a person or institution
stereotype	typical characteristics of a category of person (e.g. British army officers), often used for mockery

Questions & Answers

Essay questions, specimen plans and notes

Coursework titles

There are many possible titles appropriate for coursework assignments; the following are some suggestions:

1 '*Captain Corelli's Mandolin* evokes powerful emotions in the reader.' Examine this statement, bringing out the methods of presentation de Bernières uses in the novel, and their possible impact on the reader.

2 How does de Bernières present and explore Pelagia's predicament in *Captain Corelli's Mandolin?*

3 '*Captain Corelli's Mandolin* is a powerful political satire but an unsatisfactory novel.' What is your response to this evaluation?

4 'It is honour that breathes life into a corpse when evil times have passed.' Discuss the presentation of the concept of honour and its role in the plot and themes of *Captain Corelli's Mandolin.*

5 In what ways and to what effect does de Bernières use the idea of the significance of the past in *Captain Corelli's Mandolin?*

6 'The Italians are doomed to be juvenile for a lifetime.' Examine the presentation of the Italians in *Captain Corelli's Mandolin.*

7 'It is the camera's eye which is the modern way of telling a story.' Using this statement as your starting point, explore de Bernières' narrative methods in *Captain Corelli's Mandolin.*

8 What is the effect of the tension between fact and fiction in de Bernières' *Captain Corelli's Mandolin?*

9 'The choice of narrative method in *Captain Corelli's Mandolin* illuminates the novel's central concern with the distorting effect of the past and the present.' Examine de Bernières' narrative techniques in the light of this comment.

10 Carlo, Corelli, Mandras and Günter are all young men at war; talk about their motivations for joining up, and the effects on each of them, bringing out the similarities and contrasts in their attitudes and experiences.

Exam essays

The suggested essay questions which follow can be used for planning practice and/or full essay writing, for classroom timed exam practice or for homework.

Many have been previously set by the different exam boards for various specifi-cations. In each of the three sections below you will find essay titles with sugges-tions for ideas to include in a plan, and some with examiner notes and guidance on how to approach the question. Three of the questions are provided with sample student answers.

Whole-text questions — open text

1 **'Interpretations of sexuality and the exploration of gender roles are an intrinsic element of *Captain Corelli's Mandolin*.' Discuss the portrayal of women and men in the novel, supporting your argument with detailed analysis of both.**

Possible ideas to include in a plan
- life in novel divided into domestic and public spheres: kitchen/coffee shop, travel/home, according to gender
- several little girls and female animals to suggest vulnerability and pathos of Cephallonia
- four young men become soldiers and victims
- male characters linked to Odysseus for comparison
- traditional Greek manhood defined as ability to protect women, assert ownership, prove endurance, win battles
- motherland is a female to fight for, associated with Virgin Mary
- rape as act of violence and dominance, personal and political, by soldiers
- Mandras loses his innocence when he takes up arms
- German Nazi manhood asserts superiority over other races to hide in-adequacies;
- Italian males romantic lovers of wine, women and song, seductively attractive but perhaps irresponsible and immature?
- Carlo represents the anguish and fate of homosexuals at the time
- Platonic ideal of brotherhood and sacrifice made homosexuality acceptable in ancient world
- women despised or rejected if husbandless and ugly (Drosoula) or not virgins
- no professional women in Greece in 1940s and over-education makes them unmarriageable ('I should have brought her up stupid')
- young, attractive women (Pelagia) have to be amused and courted and won in time-honoured fashion
- the dowry issue – women pass from father to husband by their agreement
- Dr Iannis epitome of civilised male: intelligent, witty, knowledgeable, caring, sensitive, enlightened – his sad end suggests that he is ahead of his time, or that such men will inevitably become the victims of resentful aggressors and barbaric 'hooligans'

- Corelli and Carlo have a feminine side and Drosoula a male one, so gender not absolute, but shifts like everything else in novel, and humanity matters more than gender

2 E. M. Forster once wrote: 'I do not believe in Belief...Tolerance, good temper and sympathy — they are what matter really, and if the human race is not to collapse they must come to the front before long.' How far, and in what ways, does *Captain Corelli's Mandolin* support the view that 'tolerance, good temper and sympathy' are more important than 'Belief' in a cause or ideology?

Notes

There are number of possible emphases. You could concentrate on how 'Belief' makes men act in an inhuman way – there are many examples of this. Or you could concentrate on 'tolerance, good temper and sympathy' and how this is demonstrated by such characters as Dr Iannis, Captain Corelli, Carlo Guercio, Drosoula – and others. To earn high marks, you should aim to explore the contrast between the two ideas ('Belief' and 'kindness').

3 *Captain Corelli's Mandolin* covers a period of fifty years of political, social and geographical upheaval. How successful do you think it is as a 'history' of this period?

Notes

This task asks you for a personal judgement on a central but perhaps not obvious question about the book (AO4). In answering this question, you need to consider what impact evaluating the novel in terms of its historical and literary contexts has had on your view of the book's effectiveness (AO5ii). Aim to demonstrate:

- assured presentation of cogent arguments, using appropriate terminology (AO1)
- independent opinions on the success of *Captain Corelli's Mandolin* as a 'history', with a sophisticated sense of what this might mean, and judgements of its merits assessed in other terms, formed by your own reading of the novel and informed by different interpretations by other readers (AO4)
- a real appreciation of the influence of historical and political perspectives on your reading of the novel, noting characteristic attitudes of the context in which the novel was written (London, 1994) and in which it is set (Cephallonia 1941–90s) and commenting on the possible tension between these two and between these and your own present-day and other perspectives (gender, political, cultural) (AO5ii)

Possible ideas to include in a plan

- discuss criteria of 'success': reader enjoyment? being able to identify with people and place? apparent realism? wide coverage of this period?
- define common understanding of history and how it is contradictorily defined in novel and the different perspectives of nationality, geography and period
- reference to postmodernist text and its own undermining of certainties
- use of mixture of historical and fictional figures
- relationship between history and fiction – and myth (Odyssey links) and of characters in novel who transcend these boundaries
- differing views by different readers (Greeks don't accept it) and gender issues
- official history male, 'big man's' version of events, not anecdotes of the 'little men'
- note all the ways in which history can be and is recorded in the novel, e.g. music, photos, letters
- role of festivals and anniversaries in the life of Cephallonia
- novel records changes of fashions and attitudes, e.g. Corelli's comment at end about 'tainted goods' – 'Thank God we are not so stupid now'
- but 'History Itself Was Impossible' so no novel could be fully successful

4 **From your reading of *Captain Corelli's Mandolin*, how appropriate would you say the musical reference in the title is?**

Notes

For this question, you need to produce an independent judgement based on a detailed reading of the novel (AO5ii). You also need to evaluate the different contextual influences that may affect your response to the question of the significance of the mandolin as the controlling image of the novel (AO5ii). You should aim to:

- develop a convincingly presented argument, fluently and accurately written and with appropriate terminology used to good effect (AO1)
- demonstrate an individual and carefully considered judgement on the significance of the mandolin as the defining image of the novel, taking other possible views into account (AO4)
- evaluate perceptively other literary, cultural and historical contextual influences that may bear on the final judgement (AO5ii)

Possible ideas to include in a plan

- author plays and has a passion for the mandolin and hoped the novel would cause a revival
- eponymous hero joined to his mandolin in title as inseparable concept; name of mandolin and symbol of strings for heartstrings

- links Corelli to Orpheus and Odysseus and introduces general importance of music and muses in mythology
- fixes novel in the romance tradition of love being inspired through music and the rule of the heart over the head
- 'Pelagia's March' synthesis of love and war; Corelli's way of wooing her twice
- in war context mandolin represents civilised virtues of harmony, calm and beauty; the aspirations of the human spirit and the arts as the pinnacle of human achievement
- mandolin a contrast to the guns mentioned in the novel, composition an antidote to the engines of destruction
- the ability of music to cross national, historical and geographical boundaries
- music as a commentary on and parallel to action and mood, and therefore a narrative device
- a form of recording history which endures
- link with women and Pelagia who is described as a mandolin, i.e. a force for good and redemption
- music is Corelli's salvation in a medical sense
- link with Dr Iannis as having a passion, obsession, a gift for making people feel better which binds others to them and raises them to sainthood in a novel about miracles
- music is a miracle which cannot be explained rationally
- links with motorbike as another finely-tuned instrument of regularity of rhythm, ability to 'transport', arouse passion and the idea of freedom
- brings out human and individual side of the 'good Nazi' as an antidote to his uniform and uniformity of ideology – his records and gramophone go into the historical cachette
- music is a way of staving off the madness of historical necessity and the suffering of the little men
- links with relationship with animals, Psipsina sleeps on sheets of music and cats like mandolins
- 'Let's sing boys' says Corelli on their way to death – music as act of independence and rebellion
- novel ends with inspiration for concerto to celebrate 'eternal spirit of Greece' and human nature

Further questions

5 Discuss the claim that the novel of *Captain Corelli's Mandolin* could itself be described as 'an emotional and intellectual odyssey'.

6 Do you agree that de Bernières intends Mandras in *Captain Corelli's Mandolin* to be unlikeable?

7 'The ultimate truth is that history ought to consist only of the anecdotes of the little people who are caught up in it.' How is this belief made clear in *Captain Corelli's Mandolin*?

8 'Everything connected to everything else in the most elaborate, devious, and elegant ways.' How is this view of life portrayed in *Captain Corelli's Mandolin*, and could the novel itself be described in these terms?

9 'Human nature was fundamentally irrational to the point of insanity.' How is this exemplified in *Captain Corelli's Mandolin*, and what is the role of madness generally in the novel?

10 George Bernard Shaw said that 'We learn from history that man can never learn anything from history.' Do you agree that this is what *Captain Corelli's Mandolin* is saying about history?

11 'It would be wrong to see this novel as an attack on any particular nation; it is rather an attack on war and the barbarism war inevitably brings with it.' How far do you accept this assertion?

12 'All the stories presented in the novel are exposed as inadequate representations of reality.' Explore this claim with reference to a variety of narratives.

13 'Youth withers on the branch. Love turns to dust. Beauty is barren.' Is this an adequate summary of the reality of war as presented in *Captain Corelli's Mandolin*?

14 '...the spirit of Carlo Guercio shall live in the light as long as we have tongues to speak of him and tales to tell our friends.' What contribution does de Bernières' portrayal of Carlo have on the total effect of the novel?

15 Pelagia, with the aid of her father's spirit, writes about Cephallonia's 'impossible weight of memory'. What do you think this refers to, and what is the role of memory in *Captain Corelli's Mandolin*?
(Note: a sample answer is provided for this question.)

Passage-based questions: prescribed

Examiners advise that reference to the rest of the work should be as much as 60% of the essay even for a passage-based question. Focus closely on the passage(s) but also relate their content and/or language to elsewhere in the novel, backwards and forwards, and link your comments to the overall themes and/or structure of the novel. Start by placing the passage in its context and summarising the situation. Include references to character, event, theme and language, and ask how the episode modifies or adds to our understanding so far, and how typical it is of the work as a whole. Think about reader reaction, using your own as the basis for your analysis.

1 Turn to ch. 31, 'A Problem with Eyes'. How does Captain Corelli's character influence the developing relationship with Pelagia as it is revealed in this chapter?

Notes

There are lots of elements in this chapter for you to select and comment on, e.g. the mild but intelligent understanding of the situation (as with the gun) and the games with Psipsina and the significance of music. Remember to look elsewhere in the novel for supporting evidence, particularly the novel's ending.

2 At the time of its first publication in 1994, reviewers of *Captain Corelli's Mandolin* disagreed over the significance of some of its major characters. Turn to ch. 56 and to the paragraph that begins: 'When the truck arrived at the pink walls of the brothel, Günter Weber's knees began to buckle' (p. 396). Reread to the end of the chapter. Then turn to ch. 73 and read the paragraph on p. 523 that begins 'He wanted to do something to compensate', and ends 'Or perhaps he's a bishop.' Using a careful consideration of these two extracts as your starting point, discuss the importance of Weber in this novel. Is he more significant to its plot or its themes?

(Note: a sample answer is provided for this question.)

Notes

- You need to focus clearly on the distinction between story, plot and narrative and the themes and issues raised by the narrative (AO1).
- You could take as your main focus the extent to which the characterisation of Weber is instrumental here not just as a narrative tool but as an expression of the novel's themes. Make sure that you consider both extracts and extend your analysis by reference to other events in the novel (AO3).
- Inevitably there are no 'right answers' to this question. You are free to explore Weber's significance or argue that he has little, but remember that you need to consider and evaluate his overall importance to the text (AO4).
- A good approach would be to concentrate on the dilemmas facing Weber in the context of occupied Greece and the general situation of such an individual among people being devastated by war (AO5ii).

Further questions

3 Look at the end of ch. 63, when Mandras goes to his death, and then refer back to his behaviour in ch. 9 and his conversation with the Doctor. Comment on the portrayal of Mandras in both episodes, drawing out the similarities and contrasts and interpreting their significance.

4 Remind yourself of the two chapters concerning Mussolini, ch. 2 and ch. 35. Analyse their relationship to each other and to the humorous aspect of the novel.

5 Do you believe that *Captain Corelli's Mandolin* persuades the reader of 'the invincible power of the humanitarian impulse'? Discuss with particular reference to the ending of the novel.

6 Turn to ch. 29 and remind yourself of its content. Do you see this primarily as a humorous episode, or as one which also has a more serious point to make?

7 Reread ch. 42 'How like a Woman is a Mandolin', and comment on its contribution to the style and content of the novel.

8 Turn to ch. 64, 'Antonia'. About three and a half pages into the chapter, a paragraph begins: 'The first great crisis of this life occurred in 1950...' Read from this point until the end of the chapter. What do you find of interest in this passage, bearing in mind your knowledge of the whole novel?

9 Look again at ch. 27, 'A Discourse on Mandolins and a Concert'. Using this chapter as a starting point, explore de Bernières' use of music in *Captain Corelli's Mandolin*.

(Note: a sample answer is provided for this question.)

Passage-based essay questions: selected

Careful selection of passages is crucial to ensure the relevance and success of the essay. The passages you like or are most familiar with are not necessarily the most appropriate for a particular title. Try to choose passages covering a range of characters, attitudes or moods if this is possible and relevant to the question.

1 It is implied in *Captain Corelli's Mandolin* that war brings out the best as well as the worst in human nature. Select and discuss two episodes or chapters, one to show the best and the other the worst kind of treatment of other people.

Possible ideas to include in a plan
- like love, war puts humans into abnormal state, a kind of madness
- Dr Iannis says of war 'a terrible darkness has fallen across the world'
- massacre ch. 56 shows war bringing out best and worst: Croatian's pleasure in killing and Weber's weakness; madness of friends becoming enemies overnight; but Corelli's farewell to Pelagia, wanting to be with his boys, telling them to sing, showing fortitude in face of death
- Corelli's forgiveness of Weber extremely magnanimous
- Carlo performs superhuman sacrifice to save Corelli, as he once risked his life before for Francesco in Albania
- counting to 30 cancels the Judas betrayal; he is a truly great 'little man' who earns a place in personal history and mythology, eternal honour and a place in the Greece of Odysseus
- episode which reveals full extent of man's inhumanity to man is killing of the

old man by Mandras to impress Hector in ch. 28 – unnecessary and illogical cold-blooded murder; uses innocent victims for revenge on Pelagia and Dr Iannis and to boost self-esteem; gun and power destroy innocence and brutalise Mandras; civil war particularly cruel and barbaric; brainwashing removes humanity; Mandras wants to be a god

- Arsenios, Carlo, Drosoula and Corelli become heroic because of war
- Weber and Mandras, victims of ideology, become inhuman and dishonourable, destroyed by the chasm created between those who've been to war and those who haven't
- poem-epigraph reminds us that war is far more destructive than positive: whole generations of young men die for nothing, and only a few remarkable individuals become lions instead of sheep and show altruism rather than selfishness

2 By selecting and exploring three short examples of your own choice, consider the claim that the range of viewpoints used in the novel conveys a world where the values and perspectives are constantly changing.

Notes

- You should focus on de Bernières' narrative method, and could concentrate on the variety of narrative voices – some are more obvious than others (AO1).
- A careful and well-informed choice of material will allow you to demonstrate three different perspectives and the conflicting values implicit in these, but there needs to be a constant focus on the language of the text itself (AO3).
- You need to demonstrate direct personal engagement here, but also be aware that de Bernières' attempts to be fair to all parties may lead to conflicting views of the text and the nature of his characters (AO4).
- You could concentrate on the war and the conflicting values and dilemmas facing different nationals on an occupied island, but remember that there are other approaches possible too (AO5ii).

3 By a careful comparison of two passages or episodes from *Captain Corelli's Mandolin*, show how far you find that de Bernières' presentation of the Greeks is either convincing or inconsistent.

Notes

Through selecting and comparing appropriate passages, you will be addressing AO2ii. Keep in mind that your close study of the passages (AO3) must focus on the author's presentation of the Greeks and must address the terms 'convincing or inconsistent'. You should aim to cover the following AOs:

- Show assured presentation of cogent arguments, using appropriate terminology (AO1).

- Demonstrate sophisticated understanding of *Captain Corelli's Mandolin* as a novel encompassing historical, political, emotional and psychological elements, exploring and commenting in depth on similarities and differences in de Bernières' presentation of the Greeks in two different passages or episodes, and making accurate and relevant cross-reference to other passages (noting the variety in the presentation of Greeks in the novel as a whole and contrasting the presentation of Greeks and Italians, for instance) (AO2ii).
- Demonstrate insight into how de Bernières exploits form and language (overall structure, internal monologues, dialogue, vocabulary for instance) to present the Greeks in different lights to different effect (AO3).

Possible ideas to include in a plan
- problem with question, implying one or the other, and that inconsistency precludes being convincing
- further ambiguity whether title means inconsistency between Greeks or within an individual
- a novel which is inconsistent in all other respects of language, structure and viewpoint, mood and genre is unlikely to take a consistent line on national or personal characteristics
- refer to national stereotyping in novel of British, Germans and Italians; distinction needs to be made between Greeks and communists; refer to definition that every Greek is two Greeks
- civil war by definition an inconsistency, and the barbarians are within
- Stamatis and Kokolios die in each other's arms, 'the very image of Greece itself', i.e. political differences
- two episodes for arguing that the presentation isn't consistent could be:
  (1) Feast of Gerasimos, a pastoral idyll when everyone, including Mandras, is full of innocent joy and love for fellow men.
  (2) 'Liberating the Masses 1' when opposite aspect of the Greek character is horribly demonstrated: need to prove oneself, become dominant and exact revenge for insults. Loved ones become loathed, sea-god Mandras becomes a sadistic beast. But we have been warned that he has an 'adamantine soul', has been killed inside by the icy horror of the Albanian experience. Lack of education makes him a prey for any passing ideology.
- character change caused by deprivation, grief, madness, loss, fear and other attributes of war, shown by Mandras and Arsenios (and Francesco)
- but Greeks are remarkably consistent: Drosoula, Pelagia and Dr Iannis – despite loss of voice – remain loyal, altruistic, resilient
- the enduring spirit of Greece personified by Alekos – utterly consistent but not very convincing; which brings us back to the problem of the essay question

Further questions

4 *Captain Corelli's Mandolin* has been described as an 'alternating savagery and sentimentality'. Select sections in the novel where this alternation is conveyed, and discuss its purpose and effect.

5 Choose the three most moving moments in *Captain Corelli's Mandolin* and explain why they have this effect on the reader. Look closely at how language is used to create pathos.

6 'History is an amalgam of the personal and the political.' Analyse in detail two key incidents in *Captain Corelli's Mandolin* where the personal clashes with the political, and explain how the reader's response is determined by the text at these points.

7 Choose and analyse three episodes which you consider to be particularly amusing and typical of the use of humour in *Captain Corelli's Mandolin*.

8 'In *Captain Corelli's Mandolin* de Bernières explores power and its abuse, the theme shared by all his books.' Choose two episodes in the novel which show the author's preoccupation with and attitude to power.

9 'We should care for each other more than we care for ideas, or else we will end up killing each other.' Which two sections of the novel best exemplify this viewpoint?

10 'Despite its political and historical issues, *Captain Corelli's Mandolin* takes as its central subject the material of human life.' To what extent do you agree? You should base your answer on a close examination of two or more appropriate passages of your choice.

Sample essays

Below are three sample essays of different types written by different students. All of them have been assessed as falling within the top band. You can judge them against the Assessment Objectives for this text for your exam board and decide on the mark you think each deserves and why. You will also be able to see ways in which each could be improved in terms of content, style and accuracy.

Sample essay 1

Pelagia, with the aid of her father's spirit, writes about Cephallonia's 'impossible weight of memory'. What do you think this refers to, and what is the role of memory in *Captain Corelli's Mandolin*?

In *Captain Corelli's Mandolin* Louis de Bernières argues that history 'ought to consist only of the anecdotes of the little people who are caught up in it'. These anecdotes or personal ways of recording are mainly based on memory. For de Bernières, memory is the ability and obligation to keep things, events and persons in one's mind. Consequently the role of memory in the novel is the role of history, the former of which is personal. Memory, therefore, is history informalised or personified and remembrance is a way of keeping lost things alive. Pelagia says 'when I'm dead, all I want is for you to remember me' and this is the case for most of the characters in the novel. The wish for them to be remembered is exemplified by the existence of ghosts, myths, miracles, photographs and anniversaries.

Memory relates to most themes in the novel — itself being one of the major ones. It links with love; for the author and Dr Iannis, love is eternal and this immortality is radiated by memory, by one's ability not to forget the beloved person. Pelagia never forgets Corelli and Corelli never forgets Carlo or Cephallonia. Consequently memory can also be an attempt to preserve things, i.e. continuity. Dr Iannis' remembrance of his dead wife implies a continuity of their love and this is what also happens with Pelagia and Corelli. Carlo's name is preserved and he becomes a hero through Pelagia's and Corelli's memory. When Pelagia explains the photographs to young Iannis, Velisarios and Carlo become legends while Corelli becomes her 'Italian fiancé who died in the war'. Memory exaggerates and therefore creates legends and adds to the theme of mythology present in the novel. The importance of memory is that it transmogrifies history, often in a magical way, as is the case with Velisarios or Dr Iannis 'who could cure people just by touching them,' as Pelagia says to young Iannis.

What the novel seems to suggest is that memory has two main uses: to honour people, and to make sure others learn from experience, and this is what history should initially do. Through Pelagia's memory heroes such as Carlo, Velisarios, Dr Iannis and even Corelli, whom she thinks is dead, are honoured. The Italians and the Greeks who had fought against the Nazis are also 'restituted' or turned into heroes. Moreover, the author himself through the poem-epigraph of Humbert Wolfe makes sure he honours all those 'who in different places and in different ways fought against the Fascists and the Nazis', and particularly his mother and father. Memory, however, is not always positive and people must make sure they learn from it in order for the future generations to have a happier life − if that can be so. Dr Iannis remembers the First World War and he knows that people 'do not learn from history' when the Second World War happens. Corelli remembers the Italian massacres and Pelagia remembers the earthquake of 1953. Alexi and Antonia remember the Junta and the 'Polytechnio'. People ought to learn from history and memory and it is one's ability to forget that creates war. Through memory you get strength and this can be linked with *The Odyssey*, in which Odysseus is kept going for 10 years, despite gigantic obstacles on his return journey, by his nostalgia for his island and his wife, Penelope. Mandras remembers Pelagia and Cephallonia and manages to survive the war, and Pelagia gets strength by remembering Corelli.

Memory exists in many forms in the novel such as in objects, in music, in places, in names, in anniversaries, in myths. Pelagia is able to remember Corelli when she sees the postcards he sent her, when she sees the photographs they took together and when she hears 'Pelagia's March', the music he has written for her. The place they went together, the 'Casa Nostra', is also dedicated to the memory of their young love. Young Iannis reminds us of his great grandfather, the doctor, and Antonia of Corelli's mandolin. Corelli remembers Carlo even more vividly every October, when he comes back to Cephallonia to honour his grave. Young Iannis will probably always remember Velisarios, the legendary giant who opened the trap door to the past, released the mandolin and conjured its owner.

Nevertheless, memory should not necessarily refer to an experience lived. One can argue that Dr Iannis remembers his ancestors; he knows who they were and what they believed. Similarly Pelagia, smelling of the rosemary linking ancient and modern Greece, refers to the red earth which is stupefied 'not only by the sun but by the impossible weight of memory'. Memory can be a weight or a burden, to be carried and then passed on to someone else; one should share experiences, whether bad or good, because this is what it means to be human. Pelagia's memory of her mother and of her island has been inherited from her father.

De Bernières' novel shows that memory cannot be wiped out; it is physically exemplified by the 'historical cachette' which holds Carlo's papers as well as many other sentimental valuables which are mementoes of what the family and friends lived through. This repository of memory survives both the war and the earthquake to be finally resurrected, like so much else in the novel. What is suggested here are two things: first that memory exists in mind as well as in objects – we all have a similar historical cachette in our minds except that we don't choose which things to put in; second, that history is a form of documented memory, symbolised by objects such as a mandolin or a Lee-Enfield rifle, which outlive their owners but represent them and are bequeathed to the next generation. Everything remembered is repeated; the mandolin sings again, Pelagia hears the march again, and Corelli reads Carlo's testament beyond the grave.

Furthermore, memory, which is linked to grief and guilt, is the driving force which urges Pelagia to complete her father's 'Personal History' and which brings Corelli back to Pelagia, Carlo's grave and the betrayed island of Cephallonia. The author himself has chosen to remember one of the most cruel acts in the history of man, the Second World War and the massacres it caused, by writing this anti-war novel. What people mostly fear is that after their death they won't be remembered. Carlo's last words are 'remember me' and this is the case with Weber, Metaxas and Grazzi. De Bernières is saying that people (like his parents) need to be remembered for what they did as much as they need to be loved; it is a kind of resurrection and immortality.

The role of memory in the novel is not to replace history – meaning the official recording of past events – but to add to it, in a way that the personal is not sacrificed to the political. It is the anecdotal records of the 'little men' in the face of the distorted political propaganda of the 'big men' like Mussolini. Memory is a debt we owe to those who went before us and a legacy to those who will follow. De Bernières is saying that real history is personal, that what makes it personal is memory, and that shared memories are what make a community and enable us to celebrate our survival and our humanity.

Sample essay 2

At the time of its first publication in 1994, reviewers of *Captain Corelli's Mandolin* disagreed over the significance of some of its major characters. Turn to ch. 56 and to the paragraph that begins: 'When the truck arrived at the pink walls of the brothel, Günter Weber's knees began to buckle' (p. 396). Reread to the end of the chapter. Then turn to ch. 73 and read the paragraph on p. 523 that begins 'He wanted to do something to compensate', and ends 'Or perhaps he's a bishop.' Using a careful consideration of these two extracts as your starting point, discuss the importance of Weber in this novel. Is he more significant to its plot or its themes?

Aged 22, a conscript and a virgin, Leutnant Günter Weber is a lamb being sent to the slaughter. As Corelli forgivingly says, 'He had no choice'. Fate, history and indoctrination have determined that he will play the role of Judas and betray his friends. Like his Greek counterpart Mandras, who is also naïve and nationalistic, he is personally destroyed by the conflict between the individual and the system, by being a little man caught up in the machinations of big men. Desperate to be an Aryan, Weber is an alien in the Mediterranean, with no singing voice, sense of humour or love of animals to endear him to the warm-hearted Greeks and Italians; yet he is embraced by the friendship of La Scala and the tolerant Corelli, who can see the human beneath the uniform.

As the antithesis of the exuberant mandolinist (though ironically they both bear the names of composers), one of Weber's roles is to bring out Corelli's magnanimity. With an act of forgiveness reminiscent of Christ going to the cross, and surpassing even Carlo's generosity of spirit, Corelli tells Weber he forgives him for the impending brutal deaths of himself and his boys. He understands that Weber does not want to be in charge of the firing squad and that he, unlike the Croatian, will not enjoy it; he also understands that if Weber disobeys he will be shot himself, and that if he doesn't obey the order someone else will. These are the rules of war.

Although, like Hitler, Weber is an Austrian, he represents the racist views of Nazism. Corelli, by contrast, does not 'have the advantage of thinking that other races are inferior to mine'. Weber is one of thousands like him who are the inhuman products of a propaganda machine and who will return from war with their innocence replaced by an intolerable burden of guilt. He is also a victim of misrecorded history: his plea to have it entered into his record that he did not wish to accept the order to kill the 33rd regiment is ignored.

Ironically and paradoxically, he is Corelli's saviour in that he does not give him the coup de grâce with his revolver, but he does not believe that Corelli will survive, and his not pulling the trigger is due to his cowardice and not to a sense of honour. He has no honour, and in this way plays an opposite role to Carlo, and to Appollonio, the battery commander who disobeyed orders to fire on the Germans and with whom Corelli would consider it an honour to be court-martialled. Weber cannot rise to the occasion and make a noble gesture, dare not become a lion instead of continuing to be a sheep. He therefore forfeits the right to be remembered, like Carlo, as someone capable of altruism and sacrifice for human values.

He is not all bad, however; de Bernières allows no such simple national or individual stereotyping, and inconsistency is what makes the characters in the novel convincing. He loves listening to certain music, he keeps his promise to Pelagia to give her his gramophone; he writes on the back of the photograph that he is full of remorse. The chapter heading of 'The Good Nazi' (chap. 30) is oxymoronic but not necessarily ironic. (In an extra chapter written by de Bernières in May 1998, Weber's feelings of guilt and his irremediable weakness are further stressed. Weber is trapped in an impossible situation and one which he does not even understand.) Some readers will feel sorry for him, realising he is himself a victim of war; others will definitely not, seeing him as unforgivable for not choosing honour and decency – and therefore death – rather than kill his friends. He epitomises everything that de Bernières is condemning.

Weber does not appear often, but he is crucial to both the plot and the themes of the novel. The massacre of ten thousand Italians by the Germans is the climax of the pathos and horror of the Second World War in Cephallonia, and reminds us of all the other 'dutiful atrocities' committed in war-time. Weber shows the reader the intolerable pressures put on young soldiers and what happens when the personal meets the political. Unlike Mandras, Weber is not redeemed by a mythological, cleansing death, and is reduced by guilt and fear to hiding in the church and cringing like a dog, having sold his soul to Nazi Germany. Corelli's dismissive treatment of him when he finds him again is an indication of how the reader should view him: worthy of our pity but also of our contempt. Thematically he is therefore of supreme importance, as an illustration of the evils of political extremism and of intolerance of fellow human-beings: the causes of war.

Sample essay 3

Look again at ch. 27, 'A Discourse on Mandolins and a Concert'. Using this chapter as a starting point, explore de Bernières' use of music in *Captain Corelli's Mandolin*.

In *Captain Corelli's Mandolin*, music is a very important aspect of the character of Corelli and is used by de Bernières in many ways. Music is used to reflect the situation on the island, to inspire and unify the Italians, and to add depth to the character of Corelli himself. Nonetheless, it could be argued that the most important use of music in the novel is to bring Corelli and Pelagia together.

In chapter 27, Pelagia hears Corelli playing his mandolin for the first time. The mandolin is named 'Antonia' by Corelli as 'it was the other half of himself'. By making Antonia part of the soul of Corelli, de Bernières creates a much more interesting and likeable character than just an ordinary Italian soldier. His music implies that there is a gentle side to his nature and an aspect of creativity that makes him more intriguing. This is emphasised by Carlo, who notes that 'He let his rifle rust, and even lost it once or twice, but he won battles armed with nothing but a mandolin.'

The awe implied in this statement is also evident in the character of Pelagia when she first hears the music. It is so beautiful that it penetrates her dreams so that they 'took on the distant rhythm of the piece'. When she wakes, de Bernières describes Pelagia's interpretation of the noise as 'though a thrush had adapted its song to human tastes and was pouring out its heart on a branch by the sill'. This simile expresses how strongly beautiful Pelagia feels the music to be, and is suggestive of the start of a union between her and Corelli.

The playing of the mandolin certainly provides a talking point for Pelagia and Corelli, and in this way de Bernières brings them closer together. Their conversation leads Corelli to play a piece for Pelagia, and the reader is given the sense of his seducing her through his music: 'broke into cascades of chorded and unchorded semi-quavers that left Pelagia open-mouthed'. De Bernières describes the effect on her as 'making her want to dance or do something foolish'. It is clear therefore that de Bernières uses Corelli's music to bring Pelagia and Corelli together, as the music has a strong effect on her, inspiring her and impressing her, and causing her to think of Corelli as an artist rather than as a soldier.

However, de Bernières uses Corelli's talents as a musician for many other purposes throughout the novel. The establishment of La Scala is important, both as a source of humour through Carlo's description of them, and as a unifying aspect, bringing together the Italians and the German Günter Weber. Both Corelli and Weber share their names with famous composers and the differences between the composers could be interpreted to encapsulate the contrast between the Italians and the Germans. Corelli was an Italian composer who had a serene and unruffled temperament and who wrote technically skilled music. This is used by de Bernières to shape the character of Captain Corelli and the Italians who are all calm and relaxed. However, Weber was a Germanic composer who wrote the opera *Der Freischütz*, which means the marksman, and which is particularly characteristic of Günter as he has to shoot his Italian friends at the end of the novel. Therefore de Bernières makes great use of their names to show the differences between them.

The meetings of La Scala reflect the situation on the island, as when the Italians and Germans are not fighting the island is fairly serene and so La Scala is able to meet and sing happily and contentedly. However, when war starts to threaten the island, the presence of music diminishes: 'La Scala did not meet anymore at the doctor's house, and in the town square the music of the military band became ragged and mournful'. The desperation of the worsening situation is emphasised by the fact that Corelli even has to stop playing his mandolin.

Whilst de Bernières uses the presence of music to indicate the mood on the island, which associates music to the happy times in the novel, it is also used to generate pathos and poignancy when the Italians are sent to die. Corelli instructs Carlo to sing, the effect of which is described by de Bernières in an extremely moving way: 'something that came trickling out of his own soul, and it was beautiful because it was docile and lyrical'. Here de Bernières shows music to act as a distraction, a means of staying sane when contemplating everything you are about to lose: 'It was easy to hum whilst thinking of their mothers, their villages'. It also calms the sense of panic, creating a sad and serene setting for the horrific events that were to follow.

After the death of the Italians, de Bernières does not use music again until the end of the novel, when Iannis is learning to play the mandolin, and Corelli returns, having become a world-renowned mandolin player. This succeeds in reinstating the same feeling of happiness that occurred in the middle of the novel, when Corelli was free to play and La Scala able to meet. It creates a sense of completion, and returning to rights, and it is particularly relevant as there is almost a repeat of the seduction scene in chapter 27, as Corelli gives Pelagia a tape to listen to which arouses many memories and emotions: 'as the music flooded her mind, a maelstrom of memories was awakened'. Therefore de Bernières uses music to bring Corelli and Pelagia together again, and to reconcile them.

Therefore, de Bernières uses music in a great variety of ways throughout the novel, as a means of representing harmony, union and happiness, as well as for creating a powerful sense of sorrow and pathos.

(Reproduced by kind permission of OCR)

Further study

The internet

A remarkable set of resources elucidating many aspects of the novel may be found at http://www.geocities.com/SoHo/Nook/1082/louis_de_bernieres _page.html

For information on the island of Cephallonia there are several sites which provide tourist information and island guides:
http://www.geocities.com/Athens/Agora/6062/ is a good introduction, including a detailed account of the battle on the island at http://www.geocities.com/Athens/Agora/6062/travelogues/conflict.html
Another is at http://www.chez.com/lionelv/elements/english/menu.html
and another: http://www.hri.org/infoxenios/english/ionian/kefalonia/

There are many excellent websites on Greek mythology. A superb collection of biographies of Greek mythological characters by Carlos Parada is to be found at http://homepage.mac.com/cparada/GML/Biographies.html

A very useful chronology of the Mediterranean war up to March 1941 is at http://navismagazine.com/demo/med-2/chronology.htm

A detailed history of the Greek–Italian war is at http://members.aol.com/_ht_a/balkandave/greece40.htm

There is an excellent site reconstructing the fate of the Acqui Division at http://www.cefalonia.it/veritas/door/. It's in Italian, but the images and historical documents are fascinating in their own right. The contents are summarised in English at http://www.italystl.com/ra/197.htm

A semi-official US Army history of the Italian–German occupation of Greece and the Balkans is at http://www.army.mil/cmh-pg/books/wwii/antiguer-ops/ag-balkan.htm and contains detailed accounts of the actions of the *andarte* groups.

There are huge numbers of sites relating to the film of the book. The official site is at www.captain-corellis-mandolin.com and includes many stills from the film as well as memorable parts of the soundtrack.

To follow the debate on the relationship between the book and the film, try any of the following newspaper sites and search for '*Captain Corelli's Mandolin*':
www.thetimes.co.uk; www.guardian.co.uk; www.independent.co.uk
www.telegraph.co.uk

A search employing any good search engine, for, say, 'Corelli+Mandolin', will return upwards of 49,000 pages, but a large proportion of these of course relate to the film. The Google search site (www.google.com) remains one of the most reliable. A word of warning: the internet is a highly volatile place, and sites come and go with bewildering rapidity. Links lists become out of date very quickly, but if you try a site and are disappointed by an error message, move on; there will be many more sites, and the quality is generally improving with the passing of time. There is also a tendency to charge for content which was once free. It is hard to judge before parting with money, but often similar material can be found free if you are patient and thorough in your use of search engines.

The extra chapter

In May 1998 the *Sunday Times* published a new chapter of *Captain Corelli's Mandolin*. It falls between chapters 61 and 62. Since this chapter does not appear in any of the published versions of the novel, you cannot quote from it or use it as the basis of arguments in your essays. If it is relevant to your title, however, you should feel free to mention that you are aware of its existence. It confirms that there is a controversy surrounding readers' differing interpretations of the character of Weber, and also lends further weight to the theme of the impossibility of history being conclusive and definitive, since there is always more that we do not know. The fact that de Bernières felt moved to write the extra chapter suggests that he feels there may be some ambiguity in the original text. It may be found at **http://www.suntimes.co.za/1998/05/24/lifestyle/life02.htm**

Film

The film *Mediterraneo* (1991, directed by Gabriele Salvatores, available on video) is thought by many to be a possible source for *Captain Corelli's Mandolin*; it depicts a group of Italian soldiers occupying a Greek island during the Second World War who become very friendly with the inhabitants.

The film of *Captain Corelli's Mandolin* (2001, directed by John Madden, available on DVD or video) takes liberties with the plot but is visually very attractive and gives a useful impression of Cephallonia at the time.

Further reading

There are many translations and summaries of Homer's *Odyssey*. Most have an introduction to help students to understand the mythological context. Mussolini and Italian Fascism are studied in most GCSE Modern World History courses and many books are available. Greece in the twentieth century is much less well served, but *Modern Greece* (C. M. Woodhouse, Faber, 1977) or *A Short History of Modern Greece* (Richard Clogg, Cambridge University Press, 1979) may be found in libraries. The internet is the best source for the Italian occupation and the Second World War.

The White Flag by Marcello Venturi is a 1960s Italian novel based on the story of a real Italian soldier on Cephallonia called Pampaloni, and is an acknowledged source for *Captain Corelli's Mandolin*, whose plot resembles that of the earlier novel, though de Bernières claims he had already planned his novel before he read it.

Some interesting newspaper articles which are still available:

Guardian article on Humbert Wolfe:
http://www.guardian.co.uk/Archive/Article/0,4273,3850496,00.html

Guardian article on the novel:
http://www.guardian.co.uk/weekend/story/0,3605,348081,00.html